— YOU —
D.E.C.I.D.E.

A 6-STEP ACTION PLAN TO BECOMING THE HERO OF YOUR OWN LIFE.

Live life to the fullest.
Be your own hero.
Every day is a blessing!

STEPHEN EMT

Stephen Emt

ISBN: 978-1-7356177-0-1

Printed in the United States of America.

Cover was done by 99 Designs
Interior Design by FormattedBooks.com

"Our greatest glory is not in never falling,
but in rising every time we fall."
Confucius

Special Offer

"Give me six hours to chop down a tree and I will
spend the first four sharpening the axe."
Abraham Lincoln

In order to be successful, you need a plan. Most of us realize that. But where do we start? How do we know what to focus on in the process? Let me show you the way!

To get your FREE copy of the "Create Your Plan" workbook, simply go to https://www.subscribepage.com/youdecide and download it today.

CONTENTS

FOREWORD

As a teacher and a coach, I have been involved in secondary and higher education for over 55 years.

During that time, I was able to watch young people handle life's journeys. I also experienced my own personal challenges much like the author of this book. The early death of my father, leaving college for 2 years to help our family of seven because my mother was sick, showed me a difficult side to life.

Steve also saw that side when he lost his dad and had to leave West Point. He came to UCONN and found a place on the UCONN basketball team. But the automobile accident that left him paralyzed and the loss of his mother was a cruel fate for anyone!

I got to know Steve as a player and a person. That was 28 years ago and through all these years I have watched Steve grow and win the game of life. He graduated from college, became a middle school teacher and high school coach, an inspirational speaker and represented the USA as an athlete at 2018 PyeongChang Paralympic games. Steve's book *You D.E.C.I.D.E.* is a firsthand account how each of us can win the day! It is written on how all of us can overcome the difficulties of life and use them as motivations not roadblocks. It is with great pleasure and pride that I recommend this book as a guide to life's journeys and becoming the hero of your own life.

Jim Calhoun
3-time College Basketball National Championship Coach
2005 Naismith Basketball Hall of Fame Inductee

PART I: MEMOIR

CHAPTER 1

WHO IS YOUR HERO?

"Hard times don't create heroes. It is during the hard
times when the 'hero' within us is revealed."
Bob Riley

Who is your hero? It's a simple question. I'm certain you've been asked this at least once in your life. Do you remember what your response was? Maybe it was someone famous, someone of importance, or maybe even a parent or a sibling, somebody who might have gone through some traumatic times or became extremely successful because of something they did. Either way, I'm certain most of the time, the answer to this question is someone else.

Why is that? Why do we always have to feel like we need to look to others for inspiration, motivation, or simply a kick in the butt to get going? Why do we always have to fall back on something other than ourselves to keep going? I feel that a major problem in our society today is that we often look to outside forces to do these things for us. Because of this, we often forget about ourselves and the strength that each one of us possesses. It's in there. Believe me. You just need to find a way to get it out. When you start to do this, you'll find another hero that comes into your life. There's no need to look any further than yourself. That hero is YOU!

You're in the process of writing your own autobiography, your hero journey story. Since you're the author, it would be a simple task to replace the stereotypical hero with yourself. Look at everything you've done in your life. I'm sure that you've succeeded and I'm certain that you've failed. When you've succeeded it's because of what YOU did, not anybody else. YOU succeeded and, therefore, YOU should take the credit for it. Don't give credit to anybody else for your success. When you've failed, it's because of something that you did or didn't do. It isn't somebody else's fault that you failed, no matter how simple the task may be. You failed because of you. With everything that you've done with your life, everything that's happened to you, you're still with us today. It's a simple mindset. Give credit to yourself and not others when you succeed and don't blame others for your failures.

Every day of your life, you're going to encounter success and failure. Sometimes, it makes for a very busy day! It may be a success as simple as not hitting the snooze button first thing in the morning, or it may be grander like getting married to the one you love. Your failures may be minimal like an argument with a friend over something petty or more severe like being involved in a serious automobile accident. No matter how minor or how severe these successes and failures are, they're going to happen. But here's the key: celebrate your successes and learn from your failures. Go ahead; take some time to pat yourself on your back for that great grade on the test, that promotion at work, or being approved to purchase your first home. And at the same time, take responsibility for your failures. You're in control; stop blaming others. Don't dwell on what happened. Accept the consequences and learn from them. The legacy that you leave in your lifetime will be defined by what you do right after those times that you succeed or fail. Make a good situation great, and success will continue. Experience failure, stay beaten down, and you'll continue to falter. Fail, admit it, learn from it, and move on. This is what success looks like. In life you win and learn; there's no losing. That could be true for business, academics, or simply life in general. You're going to succeed. You're going to fail. Do you stay down or do you get up and fight? Do you just take the loss or do you learn from it? Are you going to be known as a fighter and a champ or as a quitter and a chump? It's up to you and only you!

Although you're the hero of your own story, people will come into your life who influence you by giving their advice. Sometimes, that advice is good and useful but sometimes, it's bad and detrimental. You have to learn to take the good advice from the good and leave the bad advice with the bad. These people are not your heroes, they're your mentors. Look out for them because they'll sometimes appear in your life when you're least expecting them and help shape you into a better person. They'll provide motivation, inspiration, and guidance as they pass on their knowledge and wisdom from prior experiences.

But keep in mind, they're NOT heroes! Remember, YOU are the hero.

You'll see that I've had a number of different mentors show up in my life at different stages from decades of time spent together with my mother and father, to a chance encounter with my first curling coach Tony, to a 30-minute visit with arguably the greatest basketball player of all time, Michael Jordan. All of them have helped shape me into the person I am today.

For me, the two most important mentors in my life during my adolescent years were my parents. Childhood memories for me consisted of playing ball in the yard all day with the Red Sox on the radio, bailing hay with my dad while my mother did her gardening, and camping and spending time at our summer cottage on a lake in New Hampshire. I LOVED that cottage. I'd wake up in the morning, walk 50 feet to the lake, and spend the entire day there, fishing with my dad and water skiing with my mom.

As a kid, if you asked me who my hero was, no question, it was Larry Bird. Why Larry? He was the star of my beloved Boston Celtics. He played the same sport that I adored. And he was famous. As I grew older through my teenage years, my parents became my heroes. That's not what a lot of kids would say. But in my case, it was true. They were huge in the community, often coaching recreational athletic teams every season. And if a team wasn't formed to allow kids to play, they would organize that team just so everyone had an opportunity to participate.

Both my parents did everything for me and supported me in every way. As long as I was playing sports and keeping my grades above average, they supported me in everything I wanted to do. My mother was a 30-year veteran of the Hebron Volunteer Fire Department, a firefighter and EMT. (It's kind of ironic that EMT was her married name.) She'd often rush out in the middle the night to go save somebody's life at a vehicle accident or run into a burning building. Why wouldn't she be my hero? My mother was the first female volunteer firefighter in our small town. My father was an engineer who provided for our family and made sure that we always had everything we needed. My father supported me in every way and taught me all about hard work and teamwork through sports. I often ended up playing with older kids on my brother's or sister's teams. I was the baby of the family, always hanging around the gym or the fields, trying to get into a game, being a pain-in-the-ass little brother. "Come on, guys, let me play!" My dad always allowed me to play. He treated me like I was older and held me to higher expectations of not only myself but of him. I didn't want to let him down. I didn't want to let either of my parents down. So why wouldn't they be my heroes? My mother and father were very influential in developing me as a young man. They did everything to support me and all the other kids in our community. They both coached recreational sports year-round and if a program needed assistance, they were there to help. Because my father coached me on all my teams, I often found myself competing against older kids on the football field, the basketball court, and the baseball diamond. The competitiveness that I needed to be successful on those playing surfaces would prepare me for the future.

Not until recently did I realize that my true hero in life was inside of me all the time. I didn't need to look anywhere else but inside of me. I appreciate what Larry Bird did for me as a youth. And I appreciate what my parents did for me growing up. Everyone who has come into my life, has had an effect on me, good and bad. But, looking back on the life that I've lived so far, I realize that because of my successes and failures, it's been an incredible life. And it's all because of what I did. I'm the author and hero of my story. And so are you! Next time you ask somebody who their hero is, make note of their answer. It's probably somebody else. And therein lies the problem. If you'd asked me that question today, I'd tell you that I'm my own hero. Why not? Very few people answer this question with "Me!"

One day, when you look back on your life, you're going to see all the good and bad times you went through. You're going to look at the incredible story of your life and see how you were responsible for all the successes and failures. You're the hero of your own story! In your life's journey there will be some specific times you'll be able to reference that have helped define you as an individual. I know I have a handful of them, but two of them stick out more than the other ones, and they have nothing to do with all the success I've had in my life. Not being the popular student in high school, the soccer All-American or the All-State basketball player, not the West Point Cadet, not the UCONN basketball player. Not even my automobile crash or overcoming that and becoming a Paralympian.

For me, one of these defining moments was when I woke up from my coma and realized what had happened, what I did, and the hell I put my mother, siblings, and all my friends and loved ones through. They thought I was going to die. I'm Steve Emt, the stud athlete, the West Point cadet, the UCONN basketball player. I was the baby of the family, the only one to go to a four-year college. My mother had just buried her husband of 31 years just six years prior, and here I was, fighting for my life. I didn't realize how much of a selfish act drinking and driving is. This happened to me at the age of 25, but I was drinking and driving in high school; it could've happened then. I was drinking and driving in college, getting pulled over a half dozen times, and never once crashed; I never once got a ticket and never spent a night in jail. I always seemed to get out of it. I was invincible.

The second defining moment in my life came about four weeks later when I was doing my rehab in the hospital. I was bed-ridden for two days because of a skin breakdown. Those two days were the darkest days of my life. I hit rock bottom. I couldn't overcome all the negative thoughts that were filling my head and, consequently, the negative attitudes. I couldn't get out of bed to go to the bathroom, exercise, or eat for two days straight. My questions were all negative. Who's going to take care of me? Who's going to feed me? Who's going to bathe me? Maybe this world would be a better place without me in it. I contemplated suicide. I didn't go as far as planning it, but I thought about ending it all. And then my skin breakdown healed, and the nurses brought me down to the pool. Oh, the water! I felt alive again! Right then and there, as I was floating in a pool in my rehab hospital, I realized I had to decide something. Did I want to continue to be negative, have negative thoughts and feelings, and be a pain in the ass for all those around me? Or do I want something better? Do I want to get out of this place as quickly as possible, get on with my life, get home, and start my new life? I made the decision right then and there to accept what I had done, take responsibility for it, get healthy, and keep moving forward.

Your happiness doesn't depend on your success. Your success depends on your happiness. If you think there are new opportunities, new places, new things you can explore that will contribute to your overall happiness and your individual growth, then do it! If it's worth your time thinking, then it's worth trying. You're never too old to try. Whether it ends good or bad, it's still an experience. Let's not forget that every experience teaches us a valuable lesson that we might never learn if we choose otherwise.

Make small changes for big results.

Typically, in our early- to mid-20s, we're at a point in our life ready to make the transition to securing our future. Maybe that means settling down with a significant other, buying a house, or acquiring a promising job. I remember when I was 25, I thought I was invincible. Responsibilities of being an adult hadn't hit me yet. My immaturity was showing through. I wasn't respecting myself or others around me. I never wore a seat belt when I drove and often got behind the wheel after drinking. I thought, *It won't happen to me. I'm Steve Emt. Look at everything I've been through in my life. I'm arguably the most successful athlete to ever come from my high school. And I'll argue with anybody about that. I went to West Point, one of the greatest colleges in the world. I went to the University Connecticut and walked on to the basketball team playing for Hall of Famer legendary Coach Jim Calhoun, sharing the court with future NBA players.* I was living large. I was on top of the World. And then reality struck. I went out one night with my buddies drinking and thought that I was okay to get behind the wheel and try to drive home. Remember that feeling of being invincible when you were younger? Come on; you know what I'm talking about. Well, I'm here to tell you that you're not invincible. I felt like I was. But on that night, it all caught up to me. The next couple days were a blur. I woke up to learn what I had done and that I would never walk again. What do I do now? Time to be my own hero.

CHAPTER 2

SUCCESS, DENIAL AND A REBOUND

"Life isn't about waiting for the storm to pass.
It's about learning to dance in the rain."
Vivian Greene

I remember my childhood as being normal and ordinary as every other kid's. Growing up as a small boy in my hometown of Hebron, Connecticut, I was the youngest of four children. My mother Anne and my father Eric provided everything for us. I'm certain that being the baby of the family, I saw more of the support than my older siblings did. Isn't that the way it should be? I would like to think that my older siblings paved the way for me. By the time my parents got to me, they had seen it all. That's not saying that my older siblings did anything wrong. But by the fourth time around, usually, parents are more experienced and have everything down pat. I remember games in the driveway with my sister, Chris. She wasn't as talented as I was, but she would beat the shit out of me. Especially if I won. I learned to be tough. My brother Carl and my sister Linda are 10 and 9 years older than me. So, to hang out with them when I was 7 to 9 years old meant I'd be hanging out with all the teenagers. And that usually meant trouble. But I had a wonderful childhood growing up. Yes, we argued and fought. But I also remember all six of us sitting down for meals. Sometimes, my parents would eat in the living room, and the ensuing food fights would result in peas flying or mashed potatoes being stuck in the brick fireplace. I remember hating ham to the point where I would chew it up and spit it into my napkin as nonchalantly as possible, hoping my parents would never see. I'm sure they did.

With my father coaching most of the teams that I played on, it usually meant that I had to play with older kids. I needed to get tough quickly. If I wasn't tough, they wouldn't let me play. I didn't want to lose. The competitiveness and the feeling of hating losing more than enjoying winning was instilled in me at an early age. And this is something that I carry with me every day. And it would prove successful to me in life later on.

I earned a varsity letter in three sports in high school. By the time I graduated, I was an All New England soccer goalkeeper, a CT All State basketball player and still the all-time leading scorer in boys' basketball history of the school, and an all-conference baseball pitcher. Colleges starting recruiting me to play basketball and soccer for them during my junior year. That's when my high school athletic director handed me a letter from the soccer coach at West Point. I remember getting home that evening and telling my parents how I wanted to go to West Point and my father saying "Do you know what that place is?" I didn't. But the pictures of the beautiful campus, the shiny uniforms, the rigors of the military, and the opportunity to be a college athlete had me interested and wanting to go. After securing a nomination from my local congresswoman on Christmas Eve of my senior year, I entered the United States Military Academy Preparatory School in Fort Monmouth, NJ. My grades weren't good enough yet to get accepted into West Point, so I needed to spend the year preparing for the demands that would be coming in the future: academics, military, and athletics. West Point was a special place with special values.

I loved being a cadet at West Point. I loved the discipline, the structure, and the challenge of everything that was thrown at me. The athletics were tough and the academics were tougher. But the hazing? Without being there, it was difficult to understand. The first night of my plēbe (freshman) year at West Point, I needed to use the restroom. Which was located directly across from my barracks room. I opened the door, went into the hallway, and I was immediately met by numerous upperclassmen, who ordered me to "join their wall" and proceeded to haze me. Although they never laid a finger on me, I endured the verbal assaults, screaming, and orders, trying to break me. I loved every second of it. As I finally made it to the bathroom and stood in front of the urinal, I thought for a second that I'd get a chance to breath and regroup my thoughts, a chance to… NOPE! The upperclassmen swarmed me like I was taking their honey. As I'm standing at the urinal trying to take care of business, I had an upperclassman in each ear hazing me. As crazy as it sounds, I loved every minute of it. It took me three hours that night to relieve myself. I finally returned to my barracks room, thinking that I was safe for the night in a place of peace, tranquility, and safety. Think again. As a plēbe, that's never the case. Later that evening, as the three of us were tucked into our beds, our door flew open and in came the upperclassmen, like stormtroopers, tearing apart our room and throwing anything that wasn't secured down in a huge pile. With a promise to return in 15 minutes, they ordered us to clean it all up and be prepared for inspection. Imagine that, a task that was completely impossible. Attending the academy's prep school prepared me for instances like this. Not allowing my two other roommates to break down, I pulled them together and as a team we worked for the next couple of hours getting our room ready for inspection. The stormtroopers never returned. All this happened in the first night of West Point. Every challenge that was in my way I accepted with great pride and sense of accomplishment. What the hell did I get myself into? I loved being a cadet at West Point.

Halfway through my Plēbe year, I was just starting to figure it all out. And then, just like that, I lost grasp of it all. West Point is just over two hours from my home in CT, so whenever we had a chance to leave, my classmates and I would be picked up by my parents and go to my home to be somewhat normal for a weekend. This weekend was just like the others. My parents dropped us off early Sunday evening and started their trip home. Around midnight that evening, I was woken by my squad leader. I jumped out of bed and immediately snapped to attention. I feared I was in trouble right away when my squad leader

21

told me to relax and to follow him. My initial thought? I forgot to sign back in from weekend leave. As I followed him to my company commander's office, he kept telling me to relax. Why was he telling me to relax? The pit in my stomach grew as we neared my commander's office. We entered the office and I was met by other military officers and the cadet chaplain. They sat me down and told me that my father had just passed away. My body went numb. My hands were locked to where I couldn't move my fingers. I sat stiff in the chair. What are you telling me? On the drive home earlier that evening, my father was tired so he asked my mother to drive so he could lay down in the back and fall asleep. He went to sleep, and never woke up. He had a massive heart attack in his sleep. My mother, the EMT, tried in vain to revive him for what seemed like hours on the side of the highway. All the training she received and all the experience she went through as a volunteer paramedic wouldn't help. At that moment, my father, my best friend, coach, and mentor was gone. My father was gone.

I gathered some of my belongings and my company commander was kind enough to drive me home that evening so I could be with my family in this dire time of need. Two hours of driving and not a word to be said between the two of us. I got home early Monday morning and the following days were hell. But, at the same time, we celebrated. My father was an incredible man, doing everything he could for his family, loved ones, and community. We buried my father on Thursday. I needed to wear my full-dress military uniform at the funeral because I was his baby. I was his West Point cadet and I needed to show that. I returned to West Point on Sunday. That Sunday seemed darker, colder, and unfriendlier than any other Sunday I could remember. Standing at attention in muster formation for roll call, the same stormtroopers who had tortured me just months prior were now looking me in the eye as an equal and telling me how sorry they were. As crazy as West Point could be at times, they were all human. And they were all there with the same humanitarian mission in mind. We took care of each other, brothers and sisters. With my father's passing, I was advised to take time off from the academy, return the following semester, and pick up where I left off. Going against the advice of others, I returned to West Point immediately, just days after burying my best friend, standing in formation and ready to go. Remember, I felt I was invincible and didn't need time to grieve and adjust to the void of losing my father. What the hell was I doing there? I was 19 years old. My father had just suddenly passed away. I thought I could handle it. I thought I was tough enough. I didn't deal with it the way I should have. I just lost my hero.

What a mistake. What was I thinking? I wasn't thinking. I was feeling invincible. I thought I was mature enough. I thought I was man enough to deal with the loss of my father. I was in complete denial. How could this have happened? Of all the people out there in the world doing awful things, why did my father need to go? The denial led me to do some stupid things. The drinking I started doing in high school escalated. I felt I needed to do something to mask all the pain that I was in. I was invincible, so nothing could get to me. I was angry, sad, and upset. And I reacted the wrong way. My mind wasn't clear on how I needed to handle the situation. I didn't have guidance or a plan to move on with my life. I dealt with the entire situation the wrong way.

I returned to classes the following Monday morning. Mid-term exams were starting in the following weeks and my head wasn't into it. Out of the five classes I was taking, I failed three of them. For the next year and a half, until the end of my yearling (sophomore) year, I was on academic probation, not allowed to leave campus on weekends when others were out spending time with their families. I wasn't happy and, with the combination of my psychological state and the alcohol I was trying to cover it all up with, I was slowly spiraling out of control. Something needed to change. I was at a crossroads. At what point in my life would I finally realize that this was MY LIFE and it was up to me to make the changes necessary to succeed?

I resigned from West Point after my sophomore year and returned home to be with my family.

Being home with my mother was a blessing. She needed me. She needed all of us. And we were there for her. I enrolled at the University of Connecticut, just 20 minutes from home, to continue my education. As I was playing intramural basketball in my first year at UCONN, one of my games was being watched by a member of the coaching staff. He noticed how I was playing and noticed how tough I was. He saw that if I got knocked down, I'd get right back up again. If I did something wrong, I'd make up for it by doing something right. And a few days later, as I was hanging out at my buddies' apartment, the phone rang, and it was the coach of the UCONN men's basketball team Jim Calhoun. I grabbed the phone and was stunned to hear the coach's voice. Are you kidding me? How'd he find me? What's he doing calling me? What did I do wrong to have Coach Calhoun call me? He was telling me how they saw me playing, how hard I was playing, and how I showed heart. He was asking if I wanted to try out as a walk-on for the team, HIS team. Are you serious? Ummmm.....YES! I grew up as a young boy just minutes from the UCONN campus, loving basketball, dreaming of wearing a Huskies jersey, and here it was, my opportunity to play basketball for the University of Connecticut!

From 1992-1994, I was fortunate enough to be a walk-on for the UCONN Huskies. I played for legendary Hall of Fame Coach, Jim Calhoun, and shared the court with future NBA players like Scott Burrell, Ray Allen, Donyell Marshall, Kevin Ollie, and Donny Marshall, just to name a few. During those two years, I saw 38.7 seconds of game time. Yes, 38.7 seconds. I don't round up; I don't round down. I'm proud of those precious seconds. The practices, the comradery, the brothers I made, those were my games. I was now on the court, watching from the sidelines, having the best seat in the house seeing Husky greats and future NBA players play the game we all loved. And being a part of a program coached by the legend Jim Calhoun. Once a Husky always a Husky, brothers for life.

When I first made the team, I was strolling around campus like a big shot, and I was a WALK-ON! I barely ever saw the court! I was out all night. I was late to class. I didn't apply myself in the classroom.

Then with the guidance of Coach Calhoun and his staff, as well as some of the other players on the team, I was put in my place and quickly realized what I needed to do. During those two years, since I was a walk-on, I didn't live in the dorms. I had an apartment just off campus. And keeping up with my "being the man" personality, my apartment was the place to be. It was the pre-party spot to hang out before hitting the bars on Friday and Saturday nights. And since I had an off-campus apartment, I had my own vehicle. I often found myself shuttling my buddies around campus after long nights spent drinking at the bars. I got pulled over on campus many times but always seemed to talk my way out of it. Thinking back now, what if I got arrested for drinking and driving when I was in college? Maybe it would have changed my life. Maybe it would've changed my future. Maybe I wouldn't be in this situation I am today if I got arrested. What if? We'll never know.

My collegiate years of playing basketball were over. My mother was paying for my schooling, and I didn't want to put that pressure on her anymore, so I left school and went out to work for my own money. I started working for an environmental firm, making a lot of money. I was 25 years old. In my eyes, my education was done. Now it was time to start my life. Now it was time to settle down, find my wife, find my home, and start living. And then my life gets flipped upside down.

March 24th, 1995, I was invincible. It won't happen to me!

A high school stud athlete. I was invincible!

A West Point Cadet. I was invincible!

A UCONN Basketball Player. I was INVINCIBLE!

I was unstoppable and untouchable. Or so I believed.

CHAPTER 3

YOU'LL NEVER WALK AGAIN

"Strength does not come from winning. Your struggles
develop your strengths. When you go through hardships
and decide not to surrender, that is strength."
Mahatma Gandhi

Every year, on March 24th, I'm reminded of how one bad decision can change our lives forever. Back in 1995, at the age of 25, I made one of these decisions. The work day started off like all the other ones before. My coworkers and I were talking throughout the day about our plans for the evening. Late in March means only one thing in my book, the NCAA basketball tournament, March Madness. Since all three of us were avid basketball fans, we decided to meet up after work at the commuter parking lot and head off to a local sports bar to grab some food and drinks and watch the games. I parked my new Dodge pickup in the commuter parking lot and jumped into Glenn's truck with my buddy Pat. When we arrived at the bar, the waitress and bartender recognized me as a former Husky Basketball Player and invited me to enjoy the meals and the drinks on them. A full night of complimentary food and drinks and multiple tournament games on TV. It was going to be a great night. We took advantage of it and started eating and drinking enjoying ourselves over the next couple of hours. Things got out of hand rather quickly. And it continued well into the night.

I don't remember much from the bar. From what I was told later, I got into a physical altercation with another patron and the owner told my buddies to get me out of there because the police were on their way. They didn't want any trouble for me. Pat and Glenn helped me into the truck and we decided to call it a night. The last thing I remember was getting out of Glenn's truck, climbing into my truck, putting the keys in the ignition, and starting to drive down the road.

So, here's the point in my life where everything escapes my memory and I'm left with a hole. It feels like my life was never interrupted but, unfortunately, I hit the fast forward button to a couple days. And the next thing I can remember is a dream and waking up in a hospital bed.

From what I was told, it was about 2:00 am on a cold dark early March morning in New England. The temperatures were frigid and snow fell on the ground and streets. I was traveling down the highway about 85 miles per hour when I passed out behind the wheel of my truck. I drove off the highway, hit a bridge embankment, and rolled my pickup 75 yards down the road, three quarters the length of a football field. Cartwheeling, rolling, flipping. My truck came to rest on its roof in a ditch on the side of the road. All the sheet metal was torn up, the tires were blown out, and all the glass was shattered. A police officer just happened to be driving on the other side of the highway when he noticed his headlights shining off the chrome of my truck. He did a U-turn and appeared on the scene. He found me lying next to the vehicle, clothes all torn up and just barely hanging onto my body, cuts covering my body, blood coming from my nose, mouth, and my ears. I didn't have my seatbelt on. They're certain I was thrown out the back window. I'm 6'5" tall; something had to give.

The police officer assessed the scene and immediately got on the radio to the hospital. The hospital dispatched a Life Star helicopter. Two factors were in my favor as I lay in that ditch on the side of the road: (1) the temperature was cold, which had a preserving effect on my body; and (2) I was in good physical condition. At least I had that going for me.

When a traumatic injury happens to a human body, there's something called the golden hour that's most critical to survival. They say if you survive that first 60 minutes, then your chances of recovering go up exponentially. The police officer figured I was in the ditch for about 30 minutes. It took Life Star 8 minutes to get to the scene, they attended to me on the ground for 8 minutes, and then it took another 8 minutes to get me to the hospital. Doing the math, you get 30 + 8 + 8 + 8 = 54 minutes. I'm looking at 6 minutes to live all because of a very bad decision to get behind the wheel of my truck after I'd been drinking.

Life Star helicopter landed and they immediately rushed me into the operating room. To say my injuries were substantial is an understatement. The next 6 hours of my life were spent in exploratory surgery. My body was tattered after being tossed around the cabin of a pickup truck for 75 yards like a ragdoll. It was bloody and beaten. I had massive internal bleeding, numerous broken ribs, blown out knees, head injury, broken back in three places, and a ruptured spleen. The spleen is the organ inside of your body that fights infections and keep you from getting sick. They had to remove it, so now I get sick rather easily. But most importantly, I had a severed spinal cord. The spinal cord is a rope-like membrane that runs from your brain to your pelvis in the hollow portion of your spine. It serves as a central highway for all the signals and communications, feelings, pain, and sensation for your entire body. Since I severed it, cut it clean in half, right about at bellybutton height, all the signals from below the level of injury cannot get to my brain. Therefore, I'm a paraplegic. Can't wiggle my toes. Can't feel my legs. Can't run. Can't walk.

I spent the next two days in a coma in which my body shut down completely, kept alive by a ventilator that was breathing for me. For two days, while I was in my coma, I put my family and my loved ones through hell. My mother and siblings had to be told that they should think about making funeral arrangements because they didn't think I was going to make it. They had to stand by and watch as the priest was there to read me my last rites. Two days in the waiting room wondering if I was ever going to wake up. That's hell. I'm sorry.

In my dream before I woke from the coma, I found myself in my childhood home in Hebron, CT, in my old room on a warm, spring day with a light drizzle of rain falling outside. The window was open in my room and I noticed a cloud of mist come through my window. I leaned into the cloud of mist to cool myself off and then something grabbed me and threw me down into a closet and started to spin me in circles. You know the ride at the local amusement fair where you get stuck to the wall? That was what I was experiencing, only, this time, I saw a beautiful bright skeleton of a person. Bright outline of facial features and skeletal bones. No words were spoken, no communication took place. Just bright, peaceful, calming lights. Then all the bright lights came together at one point and I awoke from my coma. It was exactly 6:00 am two days after my accident.

What was the skeleton that I saw in my dream? At first, I believed it to be my guardian angel, probably my father, telling me, "Get back down there. Your time isn't up yet. Get down there and talk with people. Share your story and listen to others. Yes, you screwed up, but learn from your mistakes. You can impact lives with what you did and steer others away from making bad decisions. That's your mission in life now. You're a great man. Now use this bad decision as motivation to help others."

But maybe it wasn't my father. Maybe it was the dark side of my being. Maybe it was an accumulation of all the things in my life that I didn't want to face. The closet that this being threw me into was crammed full of shit, and I had nowhere else to put the fact that I was now disabled. I needed to wake up from my coma and deal with the circumstances. No more shoving emotions deep down into my soul. Wake up and get to work.

Either way, I am thankful for whoever the messenger was. The message was clear and that's why I do what I do. That's why I became a teacher, coach, Paralympian, and public speaker to share my story and impact people's lives.

I woke up from my coma to bright lights, connected to machines keeping me alive, lying face up in a hospital bed that was rotating 45 degrees each way to keep the fluids in my body moving to prevent pneumonia. I opened my eyes and immediately asked myself, *Where am I? What's this thing in my mouth? Why can't I move? Why are my hands tied to the bed? Why are the lights so bright?*

The respirator in my mouth was there to breath for me and keep me alive for the last two days. My hands were tied to the bedside so that I couldn't pull the respirator out of my mouth, possibly causing me to stop breathing and killing me.

The doctors alerted my family that I was awake and escorted them into the recovery room. The first person I saw when I woke up was the doctor who had performed the surgery on me two nights prior. She looked me in the eye and said, "Stephen, you've been in a bad automobile accident; you'll never walk again." Then she left the room. Yup, just like that: "You'll never walk again." Those five words shook my world, felt like a heavyweight fighter's punch to the gut.

My life had just changed forever and a new adventure was about to begin. I'm sure I didn't think of it then, but looking back on it now, I had no idea of what struggles I would be facing after waking to hear those words. How long would I live? What dangers await me in a world that's far from wheelchair accessible? What do I do, now that I'm "confined" to a wheelchair? I was scared, in complete fear of the unknown.

After the doctor left my room, my mother came in. Now remember, I'm paralyzed from the waist down because of the spinal cord injury, but my entire body from the neck down is numb because of all the medication I was on. I couldn't feel a thing. My mother came in, approached my bedside, and leaned over my almost lifeless body. I saw the tears in her eyes. One teardrop fell from her eye, hit me on the face, and rolled down my cheek. Believe me; I felt that. That one tiny teardrop was the most profound feeling I've ever had in my life. And I don't think anything in the future will feel as deep as that did. She kissed me on the forehead, told me that she loved me, and then left the room. What did I do? This poor woman recently buried her husband of 31 years and now I'm putting her through this. I'm the youngest of four children, the baby. The West Point cadet and the UCONN basketball player. She couldn't have been prouder of her baby. And now I'm fighting for my life because of a stupid decision I made.

The next five days were spent in the acute care hospital surrounded by family and friends, trying to grasp what happened. Visitors were coming and going throughout the day to check on me and asking, "What can I do for the family? What can we do for Steve?" Friends, family, and strangers were there to check on my well-being. Questions about my future started to come up. Who was going to take care of me? Where was I going to live? How long will I survive? These questions had no answers at that moment.

I endured five days of nurses catheterizing me so I could urinate, checking on my bowel movements, and cleaning up after me when I soiled the bed; five days of discussions of rehabilitation and where the money was going to come from for it; five days of my loved ones dabbing a wet sponge lollipop on my tongue and sneaking me some ice chips when the nurses weren't looking. They were five days of pain, intense, crucial pain.

I had visitors every day. Friends from school, work, West Point, and UCONN stopped by. Relatives from all around the country came to help my mother and plan for my future. Glenn came in one day. You remember Glenn. He dropped me off at my truck the night of my accident. Glenn felt responsible. The only words I could understand that came out of his mouth, through all the tears, were "I'm sorry." Over and over again, he said it to me and then left the room. Wait a minute! This isn't your fault, Glenn. But he was the one who dropped me off at my truck. I cannot imagine what was going through his mind when he heard about my accident. I take full responsibility for this. I did this. Nobody else did this to me. My body was beaten and bloodied but it wasn't taken. I'm lucky to be alive. I'm lucky to be paralyzed. I did this. I was responsible. Glenn wasn't responsible for me lying in a hospital bed. The pain he was feeling and the guilt was obvious.

Remember those heroes we talked about back in Chapter 1? When I woke up from a coma after my accident, I had a ton of questions. And there weren't always answers for these questions. It took me a few weeks to realize that Larry Bird and my parents, my heroes, wouldn't get me through this. This was something I needed to do. This was something I need to get through. And I quickly realized that I needed to be my own hero.

CHAPTER 4

2 DAYS IN BED AND A POOL

"We all have defining moments. It is in these moments that
we find our true characters. We become heroes or cowards;
truth tellers or liars; we go forward or we go backward."
Robert Kiyosaki

Among the many necessary conversations that were taking place in
my hospital room after I awoke from my coma was the discussion
about where I was going to do my rehabilitation. After spending five
days in the acute care hospital, the hospital staff felt I was healthy
enough to be released from acute care and enter the rehab hospital.
My family and I decided on Gaylord Rehabilitation Hospital just
45 minutes from my hometown. Family and friends would be close
enough to come and visit and check up on me. Gaylord would be my
home for the foreseeable future. The only thing that was on my mind
about entering a new hospital was whether or not I would have my
own room. It's bad enough that I did this to myself, but I really don't
want to go through what I was about to go through with anybody else
around. I didn't want anyone next to me to witness the setbacks and
the failures that I was sure were coming. Hell, I couldn't even go to
the bathroom by myself. Why would I want a stranger lying in a bed
next to me? When I arrived at Gaylord, I was pleased to find out that
I had my own room.

Right away, I liked the doctors, nurses, therapists, and everything about Gaylord; I knew it was the right place for me. It was like

their own little city. The physical therapy room even had a vehicle in it. I thought it was odd at first, but I quickly learned how important getting into and out of that car would be to my independence. I hadn't yet realized the importance of being independent, which I took for granted just a few days before. That's what Gaylord did. It gave patients their independence back. All the preparation, training, and advice they give to their patients prepares them to go home and live successful lives. I was hopeful and intrigued by what the next few weeks or even months held for me. This place would prepare me for living in a wheelchair. The simple tasks of getting dressed, opening doors, and preparing food I would need to learn all over again. And then there was the driving issue. Tons of questions were going through my mind. I would try to ask all of them at once because that's the type of person I am. I need answers! But they told me to relax and take it easy; everything would be answered over time. Am I going to be okay? Am I going to survive? I had a head full of questions.

Once word spread in my community that I was doing my rehabilitation at Gaylord, dozens of people wanted to visit me. Although I knew this, I needed to be alone. I need to do this alone. If I were going to be successful, I wouldn't have to rely on others. Gaylord was teaching me how to get by every day in a wheelchair. One of the first things they taught me was how to fall out of my wheelchair correctly. "Why would I need to know this? I don't plan on doing any stupid stunts," I asked. "It will happen," they told me. "And when it does, if you're not paying attention now as we teach you this, you can be seriously hurt." With a slight tug on the handles, they flipped me back. Like I was taught, I tucked my chin to protect my head. On the ground, on my back, I realized that, although I was shaken, I wasn't hurt. "Okay… now get me up please!" Their response, "Nope. We teach you how to fall in order to teach you how to get back up. There will be times out there in the real world when no one else will be around to help you when you fall. Or there may be times when no one is around you to help bump you up a step." I realized at that point that the world isn't an accessible place and that Gaylord would be doing us an injustice if they didn't make us realize that and teach us the tools necessary to not only survive but also thrive.

My daily trips around the hospital to all the different therapy sessions, especially the physical and occupational therapy rooms, were all filled with strengthening exercises, coordination exercises, transferring techniques, and socializing with other patients and staff. Sessions with nurses were held throughout the day, learning about my new body and how it was going to work now that I had lost the use of half of it. Bowel and bladder issues were now a major concern. Would I need to set my alarm for the middle of the night to get up to urinate so I wouldn't pee the bed? If I didn't do my bowel program properly, would I have to worry about soiling myself while out in public? In the hospital, pads were placed on my wheelchair and on my bed just in case I had one of these accidents. Was this the way it was going to be for the rest of my life? Am I going to have to put a pad on my chair or on my bed every day and night? Who wants to live like that? Over the next few weeks, I would learn about my body and how it was reacting to the injury. And I was happy to find out that it wasn't as bad as I had thought. The pads on my chair and in my bed were only for the time being as I learned new routines. Now that was a relief. I remember sitting in group therapy sessions with doctors who were educating us on issues that we would be encountering in the future. I would often raise my hand and be the first one to fire questions the doctors' way. And after the meetings, I would be the first one to be approached by some of the other patients, telling me to try to find a disabled person first to ask questions. They said, "Find others who are in the same predicament as you, get to know them, and use them as references for the issues you're going to have when you get home. You need a mentor. Usually they're better than doctors."

Like the true competitor I am, I would have been out of Gaylord in record time if it hadn't been for a minor setback. Looking back on it, it was a setback that would change my life and my outlook going forward. One day, when I was getting ready for a therapy session, my wheelchair transfer techniques weren't perfected yet, so the nurses had to carry me from my bed to my wheelchair. As they were lifting me into my chair, they dropped me, and my tailbone landed directly on the tire of my wheelchair. The bruise around my tailbone and the skin breakdown started to form immediately. A skin breakdown for someone who's confined to a wheelchair can be deadly if not treated properly. With an able-bodied person, a simple bruise goes away over time. But with a disabled person, since they're sitting most of the time and all the blood and pressure is going to that one spot, the bruise will eat away at the muscle. What might start out as a small pin hole could quickly turn into a crater. And if it's not taken care of properly, it could kill a disabled person. Another patient in the hospital had a similar spinal cord injury to mine. He was shot during a drug deal that went bad. The bullet went through his spinal cord and paralyzed him. Because we only spent a couple of weeks together, I can't call him a good friend of mine. But we did share a similar injury and, therefore, consoled each other a lot. Within a few days of him being sent home, we received word that he had a skin breakdown. Because he didn't care for it properly, because he didn't listen to the medical staff, the breakdown continued to get worse over the next couple of weeks and, eventually, he died. This kid didn't believe in himself. He didn't believe in the wonderful care we were both there for and receiving daily. And because of this, he failed. He failed the ultimate test in life: self-care. It would've been easy to listen to the professionals, to those who came before us and had already experienced what we were going through. But he didn't and he failed. This scared the hell out of me because, at the time, I thought that maybe this entire ordeal I was going through might have been more difficult for me to handle than I originally thought. But wait a minute. He didn't have the support I had. He didn't have the drive I had. He didn't have the focus and determination I had. I had the support of my loved ones and I knew that I could lean on all of them during that most difficult time of my life. I accepted the support. He didn't. That's why he's no longer with us.

Having a support system around you is very important. Although you need to be the hero of your own story, you need to keep those close to you nearby so you can lean on them when things are not going your way. You're going to need to rely on your mentors. The inspiration to get through the hard times as well as improving on the good times needs to come from within you. You're in control of your own life. But make sure to allow others to come into your life who will support you and push you to be the best version of yourself. With my accident, in the beginning, I was in denial and didn't realize that I needed mentors at this most crucial point in my life. I refused and resisted them. I didn't want to talk with them or be around them. This caused suffering for not only myself but also those who cared about me. I was fortunate to have an incredible support system around me that included my girlfriend Kim, family, very close friends, and count-less nurses and doctors, all of which cared about me. Once I realized that I couldn't recover on my own and I accepted what had happened, then I found peace of mind and could begin the healing process. Because of my acceptance, inner drive, and support system, I'm alive today and successful.

So instead of going home in a few weeks, I had this minor set-back. I didn't know it at the time, but those next two days would be the defining moment of my life. It wasn't all the successes and losses that I already endured. For the next two days, I had to lie in bed on my side with one butt cheek taped to the bed rail to allow the bruise to air out and heal properly. Fortunately, my room was on the second floor or else people walking by my window would have gotten a not so pleasant show! The brisk air coming through the open windows helped in healing my skin breakdown. I spent two long days in bed, never once leaving to get up and move around, to get something to eat, to go to the bathroom. All this had to be done in my bed for two days. Although I didn't know it at the time, that scenario was quickly forming into the defining moment of my life. For two straight days and nights I was a negative, miserable person. Those two days were the closest thing to hell I could imagine. I became suicidal. I didn't want to be a burden. I felt sorry for myself and for others around me. Maybe I should just end it and make it easier for everyone else. They were the darkest days of my life.

But then after two days, something miraculous happened. My skin breakdown healed and the nurses were talking about getting me down to the swimming pool. I love the water. Growing up, my family had the cottage in New Hampshire right on the lake. I was in the water all day. So, getting into a pool at this point in my life was something I absolutely needed. The nurses picked me up and put me in my wheelchair, being extra careful this time not to drop me. And we wheeled down to the pool. If you haven't noticed it yet, you probably will now, but there's a chairlift for disabled people that some of your local community pools might have. The one at Gaylord was on the side of the pool. The therapist put a life jacket on me and transferred me into the pool chair. The chair then lifted me up slowly, rotated me over the side of the pool, and slowly lowered me into the water. As my body was entering the water, I saw the water hit my feet. And I couldn't feel anything. That was weird. As the water was rising up my legs and hitting my knees and hips, I couldn't feel the water. This is strange. I'm not sure if I like this feeling. And then the water hit my hands, my arms and my chest and my face and I was immediately brought back to those warm summer days in the lake in New Hampshire. The feeling of the water was invigorating, powerful, soothing, transforming. As I slowly floated around the pool with my lifejacket on, I felt normal again. No wheelchair was holding me down. I felt freedom! I was going to be okay. I thought, *I'll make it through this. There's nothing that can keep me down. I'll survive.*

If we're only alive physically, are we actually living? If we're not allowing our minds to accept where we currently are, then we're blocking ourselves from truly living. Physical and mental freedom work together to provide peace. Some may even say that we need to include others, such as emotional or spiritual forces, to all work in unison. For me, the freedom the pool gave me was more mental than anything. It was a breakthrough on all levels. My transformation started occurring during that 30-minute swim.

That's when it hit me. I was faced with a decision. Whether or not I would be successful in life would come down to the decision I was about to make. I could continue to have a negative attitude, feel sorry for myself, and depend on others. In other words, I could be somebody I didn't want to be. Or I could accept what had happened, educate myself about my current situation, create a plan to get through this, and then use that plan to change my life and lead me to success. And finally, DON'T EVER GIVE UP!

So, floating around a swimming pool at the age of 25 after my life had just been flipped upside down, I decided to change my life. From that day on, I've had the attitude of accepting any and all setbacks that may come in life. Do I have bad days? Of course, I do. But I have accepted the fact that they will happen, and as long as I don't let one bad day turn into two days, six days, or a month, I'll get through it. I'll wake up tomorrow and have the opportunity to make it a great day, to get better and improve and make those around me better also.

From the time of my accident to just before I entered the water I was locked down in all forms of living. My body was physically beaten. My mind wasn't in a good place. I was in denial of what had happened and even contemplating suicide. My spirit was broken. I came out of the pool a different man. My body was free. I opened my mind to what was happening, and I realized that I needed to cope with the current situation and deal with it. Although my body was starting to heal physically, I was now in a place where I could allow my life to heal. I still was living in denial at that time but, at least, I accepted my mental state, and this allowed the healing process to begin.

Two days in bed and a swimming pool. The accident didn't change my life. The decision I made to accept it, deal with it, and continue did. This is something I do every day. Maybe I need to go back and thank those nurses for dropping me on my chair tire. Did I really want to live my life the way I was living it? Those two days of gloom were exactly what I needed to realize that I had to decide to either stay negative, just get by, and, hopefully, live and be successful or face what had happened, get out of the hospital as soon as possible, and love life all over again. This served as my final test to get on the road to recovery. Bring it on! I vowed that day in the swimming pool to get out of the hospital and start on my new life as soon as possible and that I was going to treat every day like it was my last and attack each day with the correct mindset and attitude to make things happen.

Those two days in bed followed by the pool was a defining moment in my life when I finally concluded that I needed to decide to save my own life. At that point, I wasn't open to any of the hard conversations that needed to occur. I didn't want to hear it. My negative attitude and lack of acceptance put a lot of strain on those loved ones who were there to support me and cared about me. I realized that I was in denial, that I wasn't admitting to what happened, and that to start the healing process, I needed to accept it.

I wasn't aware of the thought processes that were going through my head. I just did it. In the 25 years since my accident, I've been a student and a teacher, an athlete and a coach, and a mentee and a mentor. I've traveled the country to speak to and listen to groups of people of all ages. I've traveled the world, competing for Team USA. All these life experiences I now realize are part of a process that began from the life-changing decision I made that day in the pool at the age of 25. This process is what I will be sharing with you.

CHAPTER 5

COMING HOME AND STARTING AGAIN

"Hard is trying to rebuild yourself, piece by piece,
with no instruction book, and no clue as to where
all the important bits are supposed to go."
Nick Hornby

As the days passed in rehab, I knew I was getting better. But there were still a couple hurdles I needed to get over before being discharged. One of them was a simple venture out into the community around Gaylord to see how I would react to being in a wheelchair, how I would maneuver around and to make sure I could navigate the basic sidewalks, parking lots, etc. We took a field trip to the movies and spent some time at a local mall. Although I passed the test with flying colors, I quickly realized that the world isn't an accessible place and getting around in a wheelchair would sometimes be a difficult task. A home visit was being planned. Since the apartment I was sharing with my girlfriend Kim wasn't accessible, we decide to head to my mother's house. It was an early Mother's Day party and my family planned a picnic at my mother's house with family and close friends. Unfortunately, my mother's house wasn't accessible for wheelchair use, so we had to have the party in the driveway. Just another obstacle. A bunch of family and friends attended the picnic as well as a handful of my former UCONN basketball teammates. It was difficult for me to be seen like this, and I'm sure it was difficult for them to see me like this. For six months after my accident, I had to wear a turtle shell brace around my upper body while I was sitting up in my chair. A neck brace attached to it prevented me from rotating my head left or right. My spine was still unstable. I wasn't out of the woods yet. Just a year prior, I was in Gampel Pavilion on the campus of the University Connecticut with these guys running up and down the court and enjoying the game that we love. And there I was, sitting in the driveway at my mother's house, unable to move like I did before. No jacket was big enough to cover the entire back brace. I hated that those guys saw me like that. As athletes, especially college athletes, we tend to get a sense of invincibility about us. "It won't happen to us." And there I was, unable to move.

When I was discharged from the hospital, I returned to living with my girlfriend Kim. We had to move apartments, though, because the one we were living in wasn't wheelchair accessible. It was one of my first experiences of how this world won't always be accessible for me. We settled into our new apartment and I began home physical therapy to try to strengthen my body. My home therapist was a woman by the name of Carrie. She came by a couple days a week and beat the shit out of me, in a good way! One day, she explained to me that her husband was on the board for a local nonprofit organization that helped people with disabilities participate in sporting events. And that they were willing to help me out.

Carrie's husband Rick and the rest of the Tolland Fund organized an autograph session at a local sports memorabilia show with all the proceeds going toward the purchase of a new truck for me. Current and past Husky basketball players took the time out of their lives to help me out. Ray Allen, Rebecca Lobo, Coach Calhoun were just a few of the many players and people who stepped up to help a fellow Husky in need. UCONN Huskies look out for each other. The autograph signing session was a huge success, bringing in almost $17,000 for me to get a new truck. The weeks leading up to the autograph session were a source of anxiety for me. I still needed to use the back and neck brace. It was something I couldn't hide. Fortunately, just days before the autograph session, the doctors agreed to remove the neck brace, just another hurdle overcome on my road back. Again, I was just trying to make others feel better, more comfortable.

My apartment complex had a weight room and a pool. So, many days of my early recovery with Carrie were spent lifting weights and swimming. It was in the weight room one day when I hit another milestone in my life. The local newspaper, the Hartford Courant, wanted to do an article on me. As I was in the weight room with a reporter and photographer taking pictures, I was still hesitant to actually accept what I had done and to go public with it in front of the community. That day in the weight room, the sports reporter convinced me that his article would be read by thousands of people and could impact many lives. I needed to embrace this. I didn't know this reporter very well, but his words made sense, and I needed to listen to what he was trying to explain to me. It was time to come clean with everyone and share my story with whomever would listen. It was possible for me to change lives with my story. That day in the weight room, this became a passion of mine.

I had to go through driver's education classes all over again. If I wanted to gain my independence back, I needed to pass that driver's ed class. I remember my buddy Bird Dog, one of my best friends through high school, picking me up at my apartment complex and taking me out for the day. As much as I appreciated him doing this, I didn't like being carted around. As much as I needed to get out of my apartment and spend time with others, I didn't want to rely on friends or family picking me up. I needed to finish the driver education class as soon as possible so I could gain some of my freedom and independence back.

A couple weeks after I got back to my apartment, just as my girlfriend and I were settling in to our new lives, I was alone one day, sitting on the couch watching TV. I heard a knock on the door. It took me a few minutes to get my balance and transfer from the couch to my wheelchair. When I opened the door, I found a police officer standing on the other side. He was there to place me under arrest. Are you kidding me? Can I please catch a break? Isn't being paralyzed punishment enough? I was being selfish. I broke the law, and the police officer was there doing his job. My blood alcohol content the night of my accident was .12, well over the legal limit for Connecticut drivers. As he sat at my dining room table, he said something to me that I'll never forget. He said, "I don't want to arrest you, Steve. You're going to SUFFER for the rest of your life." That one word, SUFFER, rang off the walls of my apartment, echoing over and over again. "You have the right to remain silent…" He finished reading me my Miranda rights and finished his paperwork. As politely as I could possibly be, I looked at him and told him to get the hell out of my apartment. Suffer. I'm pretty certain I saw tears in his eyes as he was leaving the apartment. I told him as he left that I broke the law and was responsible for what happened, and that he was just doing his job. "Now, please get the hell out of my apartment. I won't suffer. I'll succeed."

Because of my arrest, I had to go to court and was convicted of a felony drunk driving. I was awarded accelerated rehabilitation; therefore, I didn't serve any jail time. One condition of my accelerated rehab was that I needed to attend 15 weeks of a self-help program. Although it was a court-mandated attendance, I'm so grateful for what I learned during those 15 weeks. The first week of class, I and a dozen other people sat in a circle, introduced ourselves, and described what life was like because of alcohol. When I left that first night, I thought to myself that these people were sick. How could they let alcohol take over their lives like they did? I'd been drinking for a dozen years and I was okay. But was I? I was sitting in this class, paralyzed for the rest my life because of alcohol, and I thought I was okay? I wasn't okay. Over the course of the next 15 weeks, I realized that everyone in that room was sick. Just like any drug, alcohol can cast an addiction over you. So many people have lost their jobs, their loved ones, and their friends because of their addiction to alcohol. I'm not going to say that I was addicted to alcohol. But I lost the use of my legs because of a car crash as a direct result of alcohol. The financial debts after my arrest were in the tens of thousands. Attorney fees, auto insurance of nearly $3,000 a year after the crash, everything added up. Fortunately,

I didn't collide with another car and injure or kill someone else. Then the problems would have multiplied.

Six months after my accident, it was time to get back to work. I was thankful that former employers gave me a job at the company I was working at. One of the first days I was back on the job, I received a phone call from the guidance counselor at the middle school in my hometown, the same one I had attended as a young teen. A student at the middle school was having difficulties finding his own way. He didn't have a male role model in his life. He was always getting in trouble at school and failing almost all his classes. The guidance counselor thought I could be a good role model, a male figure in his life. He asked me if I wanted to help out. He felt that I would have a good bond with the student. I went to the middle school, and we immediately hit it off. We had an instant connection, a bond. One hour of the week turned into a couple hours a week and then every day. This opportunity ignited the fire inside of me to want to help others. Maybe I was finding my true calling in life. I realized then and there that I wanted to be a teacher.

Why stop impacting just one life when I could impact hundreds daily? That student improved with his behavior and his academics enough to be acknowledged at graduation. It was a proud moment for me but, more importantly, for him. I started working at the middle school part time while I finished my college education. It took me many years to finish my degree going part time, one class here, one class there. But, eventually, I graduated college. While I was working in the middle school, I was coaching the high school boys' basketball team, the same team that I once starred for and was still the all-time leader in scoring for. It was time to give back and impact as many people as possible. Although the pay of a teacher and a coach is nothing like it should be, very few other professions can impact so many lives every day.

I was proud to be a teacher and a coach. But many away games, as I drove behind the bus because the bus didn't have a wheelchair lift, I felt anxious as I went to a new gym. If I hadn't been there before, the questions would arise. Would I be able to sit with my team? Are the bleachers too close to the court, not allowing my wheelchair to fit? About 5 years into my coaching career, I remember one game when the calls weren't going our way. Who am I kidding? As a coach, do the calls ever go your way? But I was arguing with the officials and found myself a couple of feet on the court. One of the officials came over to me and said, "Coach, you need to go back to the bench and sit down." My response? "I've been sitting down for the past 5 years; you can't tell me to sit down!" I didn't want it to come across as serious about sitting down for the past 5 years; I only wanted to mess with the man. The official found me after the game and came up to me with tears in his eyes to say, "Coach, I really want to apologize for what I said to you on the floor. I feel bad and didn't mean any disrespect by what I said." I asked him when was the last time he officiated a game where one of the coaches was in a wheelchair. He said never. "I figured that. Don't worry about a thing. I know what came out of your mouth was just a common response." We laughed about it and went our separate ways.

When I first started coaching, I doubted my own abilities. How can I coach from a wheelchair? Although I love this game very much and played it at a high-level, how can I coach sitting down? When I got offered the coaching job by the current coach Frank Schmidt, I was hesitant at first, saying, "I can't get out there on the court with all my players to teach them the proper footwork for a layup. What good will I do?" Frank made me realize that I had so much to give. And that everything that needed to be taught to these young student athletes was in my head. And he made me realize that I could do good. I gladly accepted the position and remained as the head basketball coach for the next 20 years. Every year, I still receive wedding invitations and birth announcements and texts and emails from former players, thanking me for what I did, for molding them into young men. It's something I'll cherish for the rest of my life.

I mentioned Michael Jordan earlier as one of my mentors. If you've seen the documentary *The Last Dance* about the Chicago Bulls 1997-1998 championship season, you would have seen me hanging out in the Bulls training room with MJ. (Episode 7…about 56 minutes in). Thanks to the gratitude of my former UCONN Husky teammate Scott Burrell, I was fortunate to not only watch MJ play in person but to go behind the scenes into the Bulls locker room and meet the players. What MJ did that night impacted my life going forward. That meeting between myself and MJ and a couple others took place after the game, around 10:30 on a Saturday evening. He could've very easily gone home to his wife and kids, but, instead, he took the time to sit with us and talk about basketball, kids, cars… just hanging out. Here he was, the greatest basketball player ever, possibly the best-known athlete in the entire world, sitting right next to me and taking time out of his extremely busy and demanding day to talk. Why? Because he knew that just by doing so, he would teach us that there's always time to positively impact others, no matter how busy your life may seem to be.

I don't consider Michael Jordan a close friend. But what he taught me that night will stay with me forever. That's what a mentor does.

CHAPTER 6

STALKED INTO A SPORT

"Challenge yourself, go for it whatever "it" may be; we are much more powerful and capable than we will ever know."
Amy Purdy

For 17 years after my accident, I experimented with a couple of different adaptive sports. Basketball wasn't one of them. I get asked all the time why I didn't play wheelchair basketball. Although I often got out on the floor with my teams and played horse, pig, or some form of shooting games, I never had a desire to play wheelchair basketball. A wheelchair basketball team, the Connecticut Spokebenders "recruited" me heavily after my accident, showing up in my hospital room just days after coming out of my coma. But at that time in my life, I was still in denial. I was resisting the situation that I was now in. I wasn't in a wheelchair. I wasn't permanently disabled. I was hesitant to find out more about being disabled because I was scared as hell. I didn't want to see other people in wheelchairs. I didn't want to be associated with other people in wheelchairs. People are going to look differently at me. They're going to stare. No, I don't want to join your team; leave me alone please.

As the years progressed after my accident and I started accepting and healing, I'm still not sure why I never played. Maybe because I thought I would be good no matter what and that I needed more of a challenge. Although I know many wheelchair basketball players now and I think could keep up with them, I just never wanted to play.

I tried wheelchair tennis. It was fun but not something I could see myself getting into. I got into wheelchair racing for a while, eventually racing in some half marathons and then the 2010 New York City Marathon for 26.2 miles. That was crazy! Never again! Nothing really stuck with me, until I found curling.

I needed to find that one competition that filled the void in my life that I was craving so much to fill. In the summer of 2013, I took a trip to Cape Cod, Massachusetts to get away for the weekend. I checked into my hotel and asked the front desk what I should do. They told me I needed to drive down to a town called Woods Hole, visit a bakery called Pie in the Sky, get something to eat and enjoy the beautiful day. I parked my truck and pushed up the hill leading to Pie in the Sky. As I was sitting outside enjoying the weather and the scenery, an older Italian looking gentleman with slicked back hair and a big welcoming smile approached me. "Are you local?" he asked me. "No," I responded, "I'm from Connecticut, about two and a half hours away." There was about 10 seconds of silence between us. I thought I was dead. I was thinking of ways to get away from this stalker, whether it be bolting down the hill or simply rolling off into the water. I seriously thought my life was in danger but then I asked him, "Do you mind telling me why you asked that." His response, "I train with the Paralympic curling team here on the Cape and I saw you pushing up the hill. With your build, I can make you into an Olympian in a year." To which I responded, "What the hell is curling? And where do I sign up?" Tony Colacchio had hooked me with talking about the Olympics, something I never thought of since my accident. Tony's wife Mary then came around the corner and joined us. Tony saw me pushing up the hill. He parked his truck and walked around the town of Woods Hole, Massachusetts for 45 minutes until he found me. I got stalked into the sport of curling. Tony and his wife Mary told me about how young the sport was and about the opportunities to travel the world and represent the United States of America. I thought about it the entire car ride home and instantly Googled wheelchair curling when I got into my living room. I thought to myself, *This is something I can do. This is something I can be successful at.*

A couple weeks later I was planning on returning to the Cape to watch a tournament and to see this sport in person for the first time. It turns out one of the teams from Canada only had three players. You need four to play. Tony's wife Mary asked me if I wanted to play. "So, you mean to tell me. You want me to come to the Cape in the middle of July in the 95° weather and get on the ice?" I arrived at the club Wednesday night to watch some of the games. And then threw my first stones at midnight. I instantly fell in love with the sport. The next morning, I was playing for a Canadian team against the Russian national team. The same Russian national team that would earn a silver medal in the 2014 Paralympic Games just a few months later. Talk about an initiation by fire. Unfortunately, I was introduced to the sport too late to make the 2014 Paralympic Team. So, I had to watch the games from home. Upon returning to the States after the Paralympics, I was instantly included in all the team activities for Team USA. I officially made Team USA later that year in 2014 and my first international trip was to Scotland, the birthplace of the sport. That's where it all hit me and the magnitude of what I was getting involved in. I got a little emotional on the ice in Scotland. There I was, traveling the world and representing the United States of America. After many years on team USA, I earned a spot on the team that would compete at the 2018 Paralympic Games in PyeongChang, South Korea. The anticipation leading up to the games with incredible. Most of the days were filled with media requests from TV, magazines, news stories, and interviews. I was asked to attend a UCONN Basketball home game where they were going to acknowledge me on the court at halftime, 17,000 people cheering for me, wishing me good luck.

We were told to pack light when getting ready to head out to the Paralympics. Just the bare essentials and toiletries. I was leaving for South Korea for three weeks to compete and had only a small backpack to travel with. We would get everything we would need when we arrived. It was difficult to believe that I'd have enough clothes to last three weeks in South Korea but, boy, was I in for a surprise. We arrived in South Korea to get processed, which involved many team meetings and getting fitted for our new wardrobe. Two large duffel bags. One from Nike and one from Ralph Lauren. Full of every piece of clothing that we would need for three weeks. Head to toe. And then there were the watches, the rings, the sunglasses. Team USA looking good in all our new swag! Specific outfits we had to wear for the opening and closing ceremonies, the medal stand, and any media requests that would come in. An outfit for every occasion.

We left the next day to go to Japan for six days to train. When we got back to South Korea, we went to PyeongChang and checked into the Olympic village, with each country taking residence in their own building. Our new Team USA wardrobe was already delivered to our rooms. The "village" was just that: a small village. Everything the athletes needed to make it feel like home. Post office, barber, athlete recreation center, media centers, laundry services. The hospitality for all USA athletes provided by the USOC was exceptional. Anything we needed was right at our fingertips, including doctors and nutrition experts. The dining hall contained a large assortment of different ethnic foods to satisfy and fuel the Paralympians from all the different countries. Seeing the opening and closing ceremonies on the TV didn't do it justice. You had to have been there. Rolling out in front of the world behind the American flag was an incredible honor. The pageantry and the glamour of the performances were indescribable. The competition itself lasted a week for us. I was used to curling back home in front of zero spectators. There I was now, curling for The United States of America in front of 4,000 spectators and millions at home watching on TV.

As I was preparing to head over to the Paralympics, I had the mindset that I needed to win a medal. If I didn't come back with a medal, my life and the lives of those close to me would've been miserable. I would've made it miserable for everyone. Two weeks before the competition started, I heard an interview between Mike Tirico and Lindsey Vonn from the Olympics, in which Lindsey was quoted as saying:

> The Olympics are about unity and sportsmanship and so much more than the medal count. We're athletes, we all want to win, that's a given. But at the same time, I don't think there's any other competition in the world that really brings everyone together like the Olympics. You can show kids what it's like to be a true sportsman, a true champion. Not just because you're a winner, but because of how you conduct yourself.

I wrote this portion of the interview out and put it on the wall of my room in the village and read it at least a dozen times a day. I made sure that every time I went on the ice, I had a smile on my face, I was encouraging my teammates no matter how we were doing and I was congratulating my opponents. Because that's how a good sport behaves and millions of people were watching me.

I wanted to prove to everyone watching that I was a great teammate and competitor. I know I was successful in accomplishing that. Watching films of the games, the announcers often commented on how great teammate I was with my sportsmanship and leadership on the ice. That's what I'm most proud of. That quote changed my outlook on competition as well as impacting my life. We didn't do well during the competition. In fact, we came in last out of all the countries. Although we were close in all the games, things didn't work out for us. Looking back on our performance, individually, the four of us on the ice were right up there with some of the best in the world. Unfortunately, we didn't perform well as a team. It was obvious even to the people back home who had no idea what curling was. They told me when I returned home that it was difficult to watch because we weren't a good team. But like everything else in life, there's winning and there's learning; there's no losing. The lessons I gained and the experience will be with me for the rest of my life.

When I returned home from the games, I was asked to attend a couple of ceremonies that were for Team USA athletes. One of them was an acknowledgment on the field of my beloved Boston Red Sox at Fenway Park before a game. Over 37,000 people cheered for us. The second one was the Team USA awards in Washington DC. We were all invited to attend the White House. President Trump wanted to acknowledge all our efforts in representing the United States of America. I found myself inside the White House, I believe it was the East wing, sitting on a red carpet that many great leaders in the history of the world had walked on. I saw the famous dish room, the Rose Gardens, and the Secret Service everywhere. I was sitting on the steps of the White House watching the President of the United States talk to us just 10 feet away from me. Are you serious? While I was in Washington DC, I learned that in the history of the United States, there have been only approximately 11,000 Olympians and Paralympians, and I was one of them. Being a Paralympian has opened so many opportunities for me I didn't have before. It has allowed me to quit my teaching career and become a public speaker. I travel to schools and corporations to share the experiences of my life, the good and the bad, and to educate people on the dangers of drinking and driving, the importance of making good decisions, and overcoming adversity.

That stranger who stalked me in Woods Hole, Massachusetts many years ago taught me so much about this wonderful sport of curling and, more importantly, life in general. Whenever we lost a game or I played bad and wanted to get off the ice and smash my curling stick against the wall, Tony was there to greet me with a hug and to say, "That's curling." Whenever I approached another person with a disability to include them in what I was doing, that's because Tony did that. Whenever I needed advice of any kind, Tony was there to guide me.

Many conversations and many words of wisdom. Thank you for stalking me, Tony!

CHAPTER 7

A MOTHER'S STRENGTH

"To describe my mother would be to write about a hurricane in its perfect power. Or the climbing, falling colors of a rainbow."
Maya Angelou

Thinking of my childhood and back to my earliest memories, they usually were about warm summer days with the Red Sox on the radio in the background and my parents working in the yard or garden as I played basketball in the driveway. My mother loved her garden. She also loved driving the tractor when we had to bale the hay in our hayfield. My father, brother, and I loading the flatbed with bales of hay. I remember the very first day I was able to throw a hay bale myself up onto the flatbed. It was like a rite of passage. When she wasn't working as a paralegal secretary, my mother enjoyed spending time with her family. She was also a member of the volunteer fire department, a position she held for about 30 years. The woman's auxiliary and female volunteer firefighters exist in our small town to this day because my mother was a trailblazer. When she wasn't taking care of her family or rushing to car accidents or into burning buildings to save lives… she could be found right next to my father on the courts and playing fields in our small town. I still see her impact as a coach on the softball field to this day as I get messages from strangers telling me how much an incredible woman my mother was and how she cared about the youth in our town. This was something my mother and father instilled in me at a young age. It was a necessity to give back. My mother was an iconic role model for me and the way she gave back to the community.

My mother led a wonderous life of taking care of her family and caring for others around her. Even into her 60s, she continued to go out at all hours of the day and night to assist those in need. Two of these cases stand out to me and I'll never forget. I lived with my mother for a little while after my accident. One night, as I was coming down the road, I saw the bright flashing lights of police and fire department vehicles. Obviously intrigued by the lights, I drove past our driveway and approached the scene. Cornfields covered the landscape across the street from my mother's house and, on this night, a pickup truck was wedged up against a tree in the cornfields. After asking some questions, I learned that a man had committed suicide in the pickup truck. The scene was horrific. The man had used a shotgun to take his own life. The truck was close enough to her house for my mother to hear the shotgun blast. Upon investigating, she saw the man in the cab of the truck with a gaping hole in his chest. Instinct kicked in and I'm sure my mother thought right away about how to help this person. Pulling the man out of the vehicle, she attempted CPR to revive him even with a gaping hole in the man's chest. Always trying to help others.

My mother went to bed religiously at 9 PM every night. One evening, I came home a little later than 9 PM and as I pulled into the driveway, I saw the living room lights and television were still on. My mother was still up watching TV. This was the first time that I can remember her being up past 9 PM. So, I had to ask her what was wrong. She told me that she had responded to an automobile accident earlier in the day where a young boy lost his life, and she couldn't get it off her mind after what she had seen. She couldn't sleep. Again, a woman who had done so much with her life, had been through so much in her life, and there she was, in her mid-60s, still going out and trying to help others, knowing that, oftentimes, the scene that she was rushing to would be some sort of tragedy. Seeing my mother upset and not being able to sleep, I simply asked her, "Mom, why do you do this? Why do you still go out to these calls, knowing that, more times than not, they end up like this?" With one quick response she put me in my place. "If I didn't go out today to try to help those people, maybe nobody would've come to your side the night of your accident and helped you." End of discussion. "Good night, Mom. I love you." Always trying to help others.

After my father passed away, my mother obviously had a very difficult time. How could she not? She was married to this man for 31 years. With the difficulty of losing her best friend, she turned to alcohol to try to ease the pain. I remember finding empty bottles of wine throughout her house that she was trying to hide. I remember watching her throw up into a bowl in the kitchen for days after my father passed away and smelling alcohol. It all caught up with her and the alcohol was starting to take over her life, so we decided that she needed to get help. We admitted her to a local hospital. It was a very difficult decision, but it was the right thing to do. She needed help. In her later years, she battled dementia and early Alzheimer's. Alzheimer's is a scary disease. I had heard horror stories from friends whose parents had Alzheimer's and that they didn't recognize their children anymore. That would be awful. Fortunately for me and I believe my siblings, it never got to the point where my mother forgot who we were. Although she would forget many things throughout her days like forgetting that she left the dog outside. Her driving days came to an end one day when she caused an accident with another vehicle. Fortunately, there were no major injuries, but her state of mind didn't allow her to comprehend what she had done. It was time to take the car keys away. She never drove again.

My sister Chris took care of my mother and her daily affairs and finances. My brother Carl lived in the basement of my mother's house, performed all the upkeep on the house and provided a sense of security for my mother so she wouldn't have to be alone at all in her house. Both Chris and Carl were major sources of support for my mother. My brother found my mother lying on the kitchen floor one Saturday morning. She had fallen many times before,

and had the bruises to prove it, but this time, it was a little different. My mother needed to be rushed to the hospital. It turned out
that she had suffered a mild heart attack. We all stayed with her
that Saturday. She wanted to get out of that place as soon as possible. The next day, the discussions with the doctors were about the
possibility of putting a pacemaker in and then sending her on her
way. After that, she should be fine. Then 6 o'clock Monday morning came and I received a phone call that I needed to get to the
hospital as soon as possible. We later found out that a pacemaker
wouldn't have worked because her heart was like Jell-O. On the
way to the hospital, shaking and sobbing, I called the school where
I was teaching at the time and spoke to one of my colleagues, Lois.
Lois just happened to pick up the phone, but I'm so glad it was
her. Lois was like a second mother to me both professionally and
personally while teaching with her at the middle school. I don't
remember much of the conversation other than me just telling her
that I was on my way to the hospital because we had received bad
news about my mother. But just the motherly, consoling tone of
Lois's voice was enough to get me through the next 20 minutes to
get to the hospital.

When I arrived at the hospital, my sisters Chris and Linda were
both there and we were waiting for Carl. My mother was in the hospital bed, still breathing, but it was very faint. She couldn't speak. She
couldn't reassure us that everything would be okay, something she did
thousands of times before. The doctor said there was nothing else they
could do. The priest came in and issued her the last rights. Our whole
family was there to say our goodbyes. Carl and Linda, the oldest of the
four, said their goodbyes first and then left. Chris followed. I was the
last to leave. I held her hand as her breathing diminished. And I made
a promise to her that I would continue to make her proud and make
the Olympic team. Just like that, I watched her take her last breath.
Then she was gone. I remember not believing that it could happen
that quickly. As I sat by her bed for a few more minutes looking at her
lifeless body, everything came full circle. Seventeen years prior to this

moment, I was the one lying in a hospital bed as she was looking over me. I needed to be the one there, the last one there, to look over her to make sure she passed on peacefully. And I'm very thankful I did. I wasn't able to do that with my father. I wasn't able to say goodbye to him. This time, I wasn't missing it. I kissed her hand and told her that I loved her.

The services for my mother were beautiful. With lines of visitors around the building at the wake and an escort in an old antique volunteer fire truck down the road to her final resting place. It's customary for the fire department to send out one last call over the radio when losing one of their own. My mother had lived an incredible life, taking care of our family and taking care of others. One last final call went out to Firefighter Emt. The silence on the other end of the radio, with the lack of a response, was the finishing touch of her life. She will be missed dearly by many people.

PART II:
THE DECIDE
ACTION PLAN

CHAPTER 8

DETERMINE

"The secret of change is to focus all of your energy, not
on fighting the old, but on building the new."
Socrates

As you can see, I've been through some ups and downs in my life, probably a lot more than the average person. And I've always come out on top. People always ask me how I got through the things I did. Over the past 25 years, with everything that I have experienced, I've come up with a formula for decision making that has proven to lead me to success. It's an action plan that you can use to manage the difficult decisions in your life. Utilizing these steps will allow you to have a better understanding of everything that goes into managing life's decisions and, therefore, come up with a solution that works for you. It's not a difficult process. If you need to make a decision, then just DECIDE.

The six core principles of The DECIDE Action Plan that I'm about to teach you are the same ones that I used to make it through my accident, my recovery, becoming a Paralympian, and many other decisions in between that I've had to make in the last 25 years. Many times in our lives, we have to make decisions. No matter how petty or how serious you may think a decision may be, every one of them must be treated with equal importance.

Unfortunately, many people don't have the tools to make these decisions correctly. That's changing right now! This process can be used in your everyday life and will allow you to change your life. Maybe your life is good now but you just want to take it to a higher level. This process will work. Maybe you're stuck in the demands of everyday life right now and you need to make a change. This process will help with that. Maybe something unfortunate has happened to you and you need to decide to survive. This process is for you.

It's a simple process. Are you ready? Let's do it!

DETERMINE

The first step in The DECIDE Action Plan is to DETERMINE that a change to your current situation is necessary. Since you're reading this book, there must be something in your life that you feel needs to be changed and you're on your way to doing that. What might that current situation be? Was it something unfortunate that happened like the loss of a job or another financial loss of some sort? Maybe it was an accident that altered your life or the life of someone's close to you. Are you contemplating going for that career change that would require you to pack everything you own and move? Are you stuck in a relationship that you feel is going nowhere? Maybe your life is great right now, but you feel there's something more that you can achieve. Maybe you want to take better care of yourself physically and need to change your appearance. The list of reasons for change is endless.

Accepting and admitting to the feelings you have right now, alone, will increase your well-being. Accept the fact that there's something wrong or something needs to be changed, and you've taken the first step toward change.

Once you accept that a change is necessary, you have to open yourself up to allow it to happen. If there's one thing certain in life, it's change. This part of life cannot be avoided. Change occurs every day for all of us. If you're open to change, actually looking for it, and welcome it into your life, you can use it on your path to success. Just a small change in one of your actions can start the process of solving larger issues in your life. Accept change and ask yourself, "What can I do RIGHT NOW to start changing my life?" If you avoid the fact that change exists in our daily lives, however, it will hold your growth back. Changing your life on your own terms is much better than changing after we're forced to do so. Doesn't that make sense? How we choose to respond to this is the key. When things happen unexpectedly in our lives, we're faced with challenges. And how we respond to these challenges will help define us as individuals and shape our legacy. The more we accept change, look out for it, and be aware that it happens every day, the more opportunities we'll have to succeed.

Success on this level of the six-step process only occurs when you take responsibility for your own life. Stop blaming others for your failures. If you continue to blame others, then you're giving those other people power to run your life. At the same time, make sure to congratulate yourself on your successes. It's true, some other people or events in your life may have had an influence on you, but, ultimately, it's your life. Oftentimes, when you look back on your life, you'll see the many decisions you've made along the way. Trust me; there are going to be many of them. Taking responsibility for your life allows the acceptance of change to occur. Take that power back. Taking responsibility for your life relates to both positive and negative situations. Our lives are full. Every day, we will succeed and fail. As long as we take responsibility for our failures and learn from them, and take pride in our successes and congratulate ourselves, we can lead successful lives. You're responsible for where you go from here.

Complaining about things is too easy for many people these days. When you get strong enough to break this awful habit, you'll see that your life will take on more meaning when you focus more on the small, everyday successes you'll have. Celebrate life. Don't complain about failures. Whatever you tend to focus on in life will occur. So, focus on the positive. The more you write, say, or even think about something positive, the greater the probability that event will occur. Surround yourself with people who will do the same.

TAKE ACTION:

- Accept a change is necessary.
- Open yourself up to this change.
- Take responsibility for your life.
- Learn from failure.
- Celebrate success.

CHAPTER 9

EDUCATE

> "Information can bring you choices and choices bring power—educate yourself about your options and choices. Never remain in the dark of ignorance."
> Joy Page

The second step in The DECIDE Action Plan is to EDUCATE yourself on all your options. Believe in yourself and believe that being an educated individual is a necessity. We all know those people in our lives who try to act smarter than they actually are and come across as uneducated. Do we actually listen to these people and give anything they say merit? I know I don't. You don't want to be like them. Believe in being educated, believe in yourself, and people will believe in you.

When you're performing research during this step, it all must lead to your final objective, whether it's changing jobs or getting out of an abusive relationship, keep your objective in mind. The more educated you are on the subject that you're trying to change, the easier the path will be to changing it. The more knowledgeable you are, the more confident you are. Knowledge encourages you to be more creative, adaptable, and flexible to any new event or circumstance that you come across. With education comes learning, and the more educated you are, the more you learn how to deal with your daily life.

Whatever your current situation is, do the research and educate yourself on all your options. If you're in a bad place right now, learn about the better places. Maybe it's more financial freedom. Maybe it's leaving your abusive spouse. Maybe it's getting healthy and getting out of the hospital as in my case. Whatever it is, it's out there for you. Educate yourself on your options. Maybe you're in a great place in your life right now but you want to make it better. Maybe your name was brought up for that promotion at work. Maybe your friend has asked you to move in with them. Maybe you have an opportunity to be an Olympic athlete. Educate yourself and all your options. Knowledge is key.

Why continue to seek out education and improve yourself? You must take education and learning into your own hands. Here are just a few benefits of continuing your education:

1. Stay healthy – Staying educated will allow you to make informed decisions about important issues that may arise throughout your life. Reading and learning will keep your brain active and healthy.
2. Keep up with what's going on around you – The world is a crazy place out there and it's constantly changing. Staying educated will keep you up to pace in your business and personal life.
3. Stay motivated – Formal education may not be necessary. If you take the approach to learn something new every day, you'll stay motivated and energized.
4. Enjoy life – If you're educated about what you're doing, you'll be more likely to enjoy what you're doing and be enjoyable to be around. We all know those people that aren't fun to be around at work.
5. Understand others – Being educated allows you to learn about many different situations and gives you a better understanding of others around you. If you understand your immediate world a little better, then you can translate this into understanding the bigger picture much better.

This step requires you to do some research. What will you need to change and improve your life? Is it financial? Is it a relationship? Is it a tragic injury? Is it career related? Educating yourself could be as simple as making that phone call to that 1-800 number. Maybe it's a gambler's anonymous hotline, or a domestic abuse hotline, or a substance abuse hotline. Pick up the phone and make the call. Educate yourself by seeking counseling or talking with a professional. Ask questions and search for answers. Don't stop until you've gathered enough information to make an informed decision.

Whatever your specific case may be, you need to make sure that you educate yourself the best you can. This education will give you all the tools necessary to tackle the next step in the process, creating a plan.

TAKE ACTION:

- Believe in yourself and believe that education is necessary.
- Keep the end objective in mind. Always refer to it.
- Talk with people, watch "how-to" videos, ask questions.
- Make sure you have all the necessary tools necessary to take the next step.

CHAPTER 10

CREATE

> "By recording your dreams and goals on paper, you set in motion the process of becoming the person you most want to be. Put your future in good hands—your own."
> Mark Victor Hansen

The third step in The DECIDE Action Plan is to CREATE a plan. You've accepted that change is necessary and you've educated yourself on all your options. Now let's go ahead and create a plan to move forward. During my time with Team USA, we have done a lot of work with Lanny Bassham and his book *With Winning in Mind* on proper goal setting systems. Much of this step is derived from what I have learned from Lanny. Goal setting is the key to success on this step. This step in the process is huge. Before I tell what goal setting is, let me tell you what it's not.

It's NOT "I wish…"
It's NOT "I hope…"
It's NOT "I want…"
It's NOT "I should…"

It is "I MUST…"
It is "I WILL…"

Answer these questions to get you started on your plan:

- What do you want to overcome or change? What makes you emotional about your current situation?
- When do you want this to happen?
- List out all the reasons that are important to you for achieving this goal. What's in it for you? Make sure this goal is personal to you and only you. If you're doing this for anybody else but yourself, you won't be invested in your goals and will be doing it for the wrong reasons. When we set personal goals, we invest more into them.
- What obstacles are in the way of achieving this goal? Time? Money? Career?
- Once you have your obstacles listed, what must you do to overcome each one?

Make sure the answers to all these questions as well as all your goals are written down. You should end up with a few smaller goals (process goals) that all lead up to your overall goal (outcome goal). The process goals are the ones that lead up to the outcome. These process goals can be defined and, therefore, can be repeated. An example of an outcome goal would be a promotion. Something that's out there in your future that you need to work toward. The process goals will be everything you do leading up to that promotion. Maybe setting a goal to arrive at work ten minutes earlier every day or taking on another responsibility.

Write all your goals down often and put them in places where you'll see them every day so you can refer to them. The more you read, say, or write something, the more you increase the probability of that happening.

When you set your goals at this level of the process, make sure these goals are within your reach and that you control the outcome. Your success is determined by how well you can control what's in front of you and not by worrying about the outcome. When setting these goals, make sure to make them SMART goals.

SMART stands for:

Specific - If they're too vague, you may be unable to determine if you can achieve them. Be specific with numbers, dates, achievements along the way. Have clear goals.

Measurable - While you're always keeping the outcome goal in mind, it's necessary to have measurable success along the way. Instead of saying you want to earn more money this upcoming year, say you want to earn an extra thousand dollars per month

Attainable - It's good to set challenging goals, but if they're too lofty and unattainable, you'll let yourself down. And you'll see yourself as a failure. It's necessary for your morale to set goals that you can achieve, leading all the way up to your final outcome goal.

Relevant - These goals must be relevant to you and only you. It doesn't matter what others think. It doesn't matter what others say. Do you have a goal in mind? Set it and strive to achieve it.

Timely - If they don't have a deadline, you may never achieve them. Don't set these goals too far in advance, and make sure you have benchmarks along the way toward your final goal.

As you're setting your goals and creating your plan, this is where you need to get innovative. Make sure to think outside the box. And take in all considerations when you're creating your plan toward your success.

TAKE ACTION:

- Create a plan.
- What do you want to change?
- When do you want to change it?
- Know WHY you want to do this.
- Define obstacles and how you're going to overcome them.
- Use the SMART goal format.

CHAPTER 11

IMPLEMENT

"Ideas are a dime a dozen. People who
implement them are priceless."
Mary Kay Ash

The fourth step in The DECIDE Action Plan is to IMPLEMENT your plan. You can have all the greatest plans in place but if you don't act on them, then it's all a huge waste of time. Make sure that every step you included in your CREATE stage is covered here in the IMPLEMENT stage. You laid out your plan and now you need to make sure you address everything you came up with in the previous step. Immerse yourself in your plan.

In this step, you need to get feedback from others: friends, family, coworkers, those people who are close to you and whom you trust. Tell them what you're doing and respect their feedback. They care about you. Make sure you dive headfirst into this adventure you're about to take. But you don't have to do it alone. The decision is all yours and you're responsible for your life but having others by your side on this journey will help. But be aware of the people around you. Your standards will be raised or lowered by the individuals you surround yourself with. They will either help or hinder you from becoming the best version of yourself. Surround yourself with people who are going to challenge you, keep you focused, and raise you up when the time comes. It's inevitable, however, that negative people will come around you. As you implement your plan, make sure you overcome these negative influences. People are going to be telling you that you can't do it. People will be criticizing your every move and telling you that you're battling against some insurmountable odds. At this point in your journey, you need to keep in mind that there's no going back. You've decided to change your life. Now put this plan into action and stay focused on your main objective. Attitudes are contagious; if there are negative people or situations influencing you at this stage, get rid of them now. You need to be aware of this and stay away from negative people. They'll ruin your life.

Is it your career that you want to change? Many people are stuck in the rut of just going to work for 40 hours a week and collecting a paycheck. These are the people who are usually emailing each other all week, with a ton of negativity about their job, coworkers, or their bosses and can't wait for quitting time on Friday. Individuals who are caught in the miserable jobs have a negative impact not only on themselves but also all those they encounter, usually adding stress to situations where there's no need for stress. A third of our lives is spent working. Because of that, don't you think we need to invest more time into making that third of our life more enjoyable for not only ourselves but also everyone around us? No matter what's happening around you in the world today, there's always an opportunity to get out of the rut you're currently in and find something you truly enjoy and love to do. Once you find that, dive right in and change your career path.

What happens when your family needs to pack up everything they own and move to another town, state, or even country? Maybe one of the parents got their job relocated or maybe a move to be around family is the right thing to do. For whatever reason, moving residences is a huge decision that needs to be made. These situations are sometimes inevitable. Make the move!

Health issues occur to us all. Is it an accident? Is life going to change for you forever going forward because of something unfortunate that recently happened? Do you have a family member who requires extra attention at this point in their lives? These things happen. Take care of the well-being of not only yourself but the ones you love.

Maybe you find yourself in a horrible relationship, one that's constantly draining on you mentally, emotionally, and even possibly physically. Getting out of a relationship like this takes courage. Courage comes in many forms, and those who take a stand against bad relationships and then get themselves out of it are the courageous ones. If you're not where you want to be in your relationship, it's time to make a change. If you love your career but dread coming home, you're not living your life to the utmost. Your entire day should be filled with love and joy and you shouldn't stop until you achieve this. If you're being treated poorly, that isn't love. If you're being neglected, that isn't love. If you're being abused in any form, that isn't love. Get out! You deserve a better life. You deserve to be loved and treated with respect and kindness. You know you're in a bad place. And maybe others around you know that you're in a bad place. You have it inside of you to do something about it. Don't waste another day. Get out now!

We're all unique, beautiful people; therefore, we all live different lives. Learn from other people. Take the good from the good and leave the bad with the bad. It's good to be inspired and it's okay to be discouraged. But don't compare yourself with others. Instead, compare your life today with what it was yesterday, last week, last month, or even last year. Compare yourself with yourself. Constantly strive to get better. If yesterday was bad, make today good. If yesterday was good, make today great. It's up to you and nobody else. At the end of the day, you must answer only to yourself. When you're looking at yourself in the mirror, there's nobody else to see but yourself. This is the only person you need to answer to, nobody else. Ask yourself this one simple question. Did I do my best today? If you can answer yes, then it was a great day today. Get some rest and do it again tomorrow. If the answer is no, then you need to find out what you could've done better. Get some rest and fix it tomorrow. Today is gone; tomorrow is a fresh start!

Change your attitude or mindset. The human brain is an incredible thing. It has so much potential to improve yourself and others. But too many people nowadays try to help others when their own lives are in disarray. How can we possibly go out and help another person when we have issues ourselves? Take care of yourself. Get a good sense of how you're feeling at this exact moment because that's what's going to drive what happens to you. Events that happen to you in your life can be directly related to your feelings. Therefore, how you feel affects the events that take place around you. Change your feelings and change the events.

Allow your mind to be free. Speak your mind, express your opinions, and be positive in your thoughts. You become what you think. If you only fill your mind with positive images and thoughts, that's the person you'll become. If you allow negativity to come into your thoughts, you won't be as happy as you should be. The behaviors that we exhibit are a result of our emotions, which, in turn, are a result of our thoughts. It's a pretty basic equation if you think about it. What you think is the foundation to how you behave. Therefore, how you think is going to dictate what kind of people you surround yourself with.

Positivity attracts positivity. Negativity attracts negativity. Keep only positive thoughts in your mind. Even the slightest negativity will hold you back. Therefore, you need to change your outlook on everything you do and turn any pessimism you might have into optimism. You'll find that by simply changing your daily thoughts, you'll attract more positive people and events into your life. So, the basis of changing your attitude or your mindset comes down to finding the positive in every situation. This can sometimes be difficult to do, but trust me; there's always something positive to come out of every situation. As minor or extreme your current situation may seem to be, always look for the silver lining. But it's not just going to happen on its own. It starts by changing your mindset to think more positively. You need to remain focused on the solution and all the good that's going to happen and not on the problem. When you do that, you'll feel better about yourself. And when you feel better about yourself, you'll behave in a more positive way. You won't be able to grow as an individual until you decide to change your thoughts.

How can you change your attitude or your mindset? You can start with a morning daily ritual. My morning ritual (I try to be as consistent as possible; sometimes it's tough!) takes roughly two hours to get through. I start off with a warm lemon water and cayenne pepper drink. I'll follow that up 30 minutes later with some celery juice and 30 minutes after that is usually a fruit and protein shake. During this hour, I'm doing some light reading or attending to business on the computer. I then do a physical workout followed with a short meditation session and some mindfulness and positive imagery exercises. This routine helps me start my day energized and with a clear and healthy mind, ready to tackle the day!

Based on your plan, make a to-do list for the following day, the following week, the following month. At the end of your day, go through that list and make sure you got everything accomplished that you set out. Remember that a goal without a plan is just a wish. Finish your day with journaling about your experiences. What went right? What went wrong? Write everything down!

How can you clear your mind? Here are a few things you can do to decrease any unnecessary clutter that may be present in your mind right now.

MEDITATION

Before you can change your mindset, you need to free your mind and clear it of anything that may be going on. Set it free. I've learned over the years that a great way of doing this is with meditation. Meditation is an ideal way to slow down your thoughts and forget about things for a time. You can meditate anywhere. You don't need a gym, any equipment, or a partner. And all it takes is as little as five minutes a day. When trained through meditation, the human brain can be taught to free itself of all thoughts and ideas. Meditation trains you to recognize that ideas are all around you in your head, but you can just let them come and go. Don't fight with them. Don't give them any extra meaning. A simple 15-minute meditation session every day will allow you to train your mind to clear itself of all the unnecessary chatter that may be occurring. Once you do that, you'll start to see things more clearly. Meditation will increase your awareness of your body and your immediate surroundings.

Benefits of meditation
- Reduces stress – decreases the levels of cortisol, a stress hormone that's the root of many of the harmful effects of stress
- Controls anxiety – less anxiety comes directly from having less stress
- Promotes emotional health – meditation can reduce depression
- Enhance self-awareness – through meditation, you can train your mind to block out negative thoughts that may enter your mind and increase the positive self-talk.
- Improves sleep – training your mind to "shut down" will help fight insomnia where many of us are lying in bed with dozens of thoughts running through our mind.

EXERCISE

Another way to take care of your mind is through exercise. Physical exercise makes the body release hormones called endorphins. Every time you exercise, a chemical reaction occurs in your body. Your brain receptors interact with the endorphins released and reduces the brain's perception of pain. Physical exercise can also increase the production of serotonin which helps relieve feelings of depression. Because of this reaction, a positive feeling is released into your body and you can develop a positive outlook in your brain.

Benefits of exercise
- Helps control weight – exercising more increases the number of calories you burn. As long as that is greater than the number of calories you take in for a day, you'll lose weight, therefore, making you not only looking better but feeling better about yourself mentally.
- Reduces risk of heart disease – increased physical activity strengthens the heart and increases the blood flow around the heart, in turn, increasing the oxygen levels in your body. Allowing you to live a longer, healthier, and happier life.
- Develops strong muscles and bones – allowing you to live a longer life.
- Increases energy levels.

ENJOY THE OUTDOORS

A third way of clearing your mind is to simply get out and enjoy nature. Whether that's going for a walk, swimming, or just sitting outside. Being outside reduces feelings of anger, depression, and fear and increases pleasant feelings.

Benefits of being in nature
- Boosts your energy – 20 minutes outdoors equals one cup of coffee
- Natural sunlight helps ease pain. Natural sunlight leads to an increase in serotonin, the feel-good hormone. This could lead to less stress and eventually less pain medication.
- Increase of vitamin D – we get more than 90% of our vitamin D from direct sunlight.

MASSAGE THERAPY

My wife is a massage therapist and let me tell you, when I get off that massage table after 60 minutes with her, I feel more relaxed than ever and ready to take on the world.

Benefits of massage
- Reduces stress – Massage increases blood flow. Positive hormones like endorphins and serotonin can be found within the blood. These hormones increase your well-being and your ability to relax.
- Oxygenates tissue – Proper blood circulation also brings oxygen-rich blood to damaged areas.
- Reduce pain – Massage therapy reduces muscle contractions and spasms as well as reducing compression of the nerves.

Although the first three steps of The D.E.C.I.D.E. Action Plan may be the most time consuming, this fourth step is, by far, the most demanding. This is where you need to believe in yourself more than ever. You must have a reason for doing what you're doing, a reason that means so much to you that you'll do anything to achieve it. You're either trying to overcome a negative situation in your life or trying to improve an already good situation. Either way, you'll become a better person because of this. The drive, spirit, power inside of you will come forth and make sure this happens. Trust in it and trust in the process.

TAKE ACTION:

- Immerse yourself in your plan.
- Surround yourself with positive people.
- Block out the negative.
- You only need to answer to yourself.
- Change your attitude or your mindset.
- Create a new healthy life.

CHAPTER 12

DON'T EVER GIVE UP

"Most of the important things in the world have been
accomplished by people who have kept on trying
when there seemed to be no hope at all."
Dale Carnegie

The fifth step in The DECIDE Action Plan is DON'T ever give up!
What's your passion? Discover your sense of purpose and source of
strength. There's something that's driving you right now to be a better person. Whatever this is, you must put it into everything you do.
Believe in it and it will become part of you. Whatever your goal is,
you've got to desire it so bad that you're willing to do anything to
achieve it and separate yourself from those who wouldn't. As long as
your outcome goal that you defined in the CREATE step is in align-
ment with this true passion that's driving you, you'll stay motivated to
achieve it. You must stay resilient, persistent, and determined. Dream.
Dream BIG! Don't ever give up.

It's very crucial during this step that you don't delay in getting
started. Every day, every step, doing the little things will add up to
huge results. Time isn't on your side. As much as you want to think
it is. Father time gets to all of us eventually. If you don't pursue this
dream, this goal, right now, your day may never come. You need to
hold yourself in high self-esteem and self-respect. The only one who's
going to do this for you is you! If you don't love yourself, it's going to
be difficult to go on this journey. Accept who you are and love who

you are. Have positive conversations with yourself. Take it personal and build yourself up because there may not be anybody else who will. But that's okay. You don't need anybody else. You need yourself. You're a beautiful person. Tell yourself that over and over and over. And believe what you say. As you do this, you build yourself up. And as you build yourself up, you build up others around you. Face your fears. Each time you do, it will get easier. Be thankful for what you have. There's always someone worse off. Focus only on what you can control. How you respond to an event will determine your outcome. Stop focusing on events and start focusing on how you respond to them. You'll be amazed at how petty some of these events are.

Here is a short list of some incredible things done by some incredible people:

- At the age of 30, Steve Jobs was fired by the board of directors at Apple. Jobs founded a new company which was later acquired by Apple.
- Bill Gates dropped out of Harvard and his first company was a financial bust. He then founded Microsoft at the age of 31.
- Abraham Lincoln failed in business in 1831, suffered a nervous breakdown in 1836, and was defeated in his presidential run in 1856. But he became the United States 16th President in 1861.
- Walt Disney dropped out of school at an early age. His first business went bankrupt and he was once fired from a newspaper for not being creative enough.
- Elvis Presley failed his youth music classes and was a childhood misfit. His first vocal recordings weren't successful and he was told he wasn't going anywhere with his music career.
- Michael Jordan was cut from his high school basketball team.
- Dr. Seuss's first book was rejected by publishers 27 times.
- George Lucas's Star Wars was rejected by three MAJOR studios before being picked up by a smaller one hoping it might turn into something.

- Oprah Winfrey was fired from her first job as a TV news anchor because she was too emotionally invested in the news she was reporting on.

These are only examples to show you what's possible when you dream big. Don't compare your life to any of these. Unfortunately, many people often compare their lives to others and they tend to focus on the things they have, mostly the material items: expensive cars, houses, meaningless items. We often forget that our lives are filled with so much and everything we may ever need to survive is probably in our possession already. I originally thought that success was defined by superficial/materialistic items. But I realized later in life that success is defined by meaningful relationships and true connections. If you find yourself comparing your life to others, stop. Why are you overlooking what you have right in front of you? Why are you living someone else's life? What you're seeing on TV or reading on Facebook isn't you. Be thankful for what you have. Take a moment to settle down and relax and appreciate what you have. Stop trying to out-do those around you. No matter how bad you may have it right now, there's always someone worse off than you are.

It starts with a belief. Do you think the most successful people in the world got to where they are because they were born that way? Or maybe they're wired differently than you and I are? No. They're that way because they BELIEVED they were the best and worked tirelessly to get to where they are. Their success started with their belief. Everything they've achieved in their lives followed their beliefs. Without the belief, they wouldn't be on top. They haven't accepted what their fate in life is; they've gone out and created their own destiny.

Keep going no matter what obstacles may be in your way. Every setback needs to be looked at as another opportunity to learn and improve and you're going to get better because of it. The only failure is not trying. Speak positively about yourself and the situation during these times. What comes out of your mouth affects your mindset. You need to stay strong and keep in mind that although life right now may be tough, eventually it will get better. It may seem that right now you're battling uphill but, eventually, you'll reach the peak and then it's all downhill and smoother sailing from there. The peak of your climb will absolutely be the toughest when you'll realize that a breakpoint is coming. All tough situations have a breakpoint. Stay strong. Stay positive. You'll pass that breakpoint and realize that you took on the challenge and made something of it. You're better because of it. You got this!

TAKE ACTION:

- Don't ever give up.
- Determine your passion and put that into everything you do.
- Do it today!
- Stay resilient, persistent, and determined.
- Love yourself.
- Don't compare your lives to others.
- Focus on how you respond to events, not the actual event.

CHAPTER 13

EVALUATE

"When it comes to spiritual truth, how can we know we are on the right path? One way is by asking the right questions—the kind that help us ponder our progress and evaluate how things are working for us."
Dieter F. Uchtdorf

The final step in The DECIDE Action Plan is to EVALUATE your progress. During your journey toward your ultimate objective, you'll reach important milestones and accomplish smaller goals. When you do this, make sure you set your sights on the next goal in your plan. Achieve one, go on to the next. As long as you set your goals up as SMART goals, you'll be able to measure your achievements daily. Make sure to set time aside daily to evaluate what you've done and what still needs to be done to achieve your goal. Make sure while you're doing all of this, you're keeping the overall objective in mind. Make sure to reflect on your daily goals and keep the big picture in mind. We all need to see the light at the end of the tunnel. You'll get there.

Recruit others to check up on you; they'll help keep you accountable. Enlist friends, family members, those in your life whom you trust. Although it's very important to achieve this goal for yourself, having accountability partners will keep you focused and continuously striving toward achieving your goal. The possibility of letting them down will motivate you. And when you do accomplish your goals, they'll be there to help you celebrate! As you're working on your SMART goals, you need to evaluate whether or not you're on track. Are you moving in the right direction? If so, keep plugging along. If not, why not? What needs to be changed? Reassess and throw something out if you feel it's not working.

Remember that with anything you do in your life, there's winning and there's learning; there's no losing. When you embrace this and make it a part of your everyday life, you'll be able to avoid finding yourself reeling from defeat or feeling bad for yourself, and you'll be able to overcome right away and move on.

TAKE ACTION:

- Refer to your goals daily.
- Achieve one goal and then set another right away.
- Always keep the main goal in focus.
- Ask others to keep you accountable.
- Are you on track? Keep going!
- Are you off track? Determine what isn't working and change it!

CHAPTER 14

BE YOUR OWN HERO

"A bird sitting in a tree is *never afraid* of the branch breaking,
because it's trust is not in the branch, but *in it's wings.*"
Unknown

Here are two examples of how I used this process to make very important decisions in my life. The first example is when I took a tragic event in my life and made it a positive. The second is embracing an opportunity to take my life to another level.

OVERCOMING MY ACCIDENT

Determine – I accepted that what I did was entirely my fault and didn't blame anyone else. I realized that I didn't want to be a negative person or to be a burden on people. I could still live a productive life because I still had my upper body, my brain, and my heart.

Educate – I talked to doctors and other spinal cord injured people, read research studies, and researched the best rehab hospitals. I asked questions and got answers.

Create – I needed to get out of the hospital and started on this new journey as soon as I could so I was a great patient, listening to medical professionals and mentors. My goal was to get the back brace off and get back to work in six months. I was scheduled to do my in-home rehabilitation three times a week. I needed to do this for myself and for all those who were close to me. My SMART goals consisted of time up in my chair and time spent doing rehabilitation exercises. I knew reaching these goals of being able to stay in my chair for longer stretches of time meant longer hours I could be working.

Implement – I woke up with a positive attitude every day and got out of my apartment whenever possible. I would ask questions of doctors and mentors daily. I made sure to use my back brace whenever I was sitting up so my back could heal properly. I worked hard during rehab but made sure not to overdo it so I wouldn't aggravate my injuries. I received training for my new role at work so I would be ready to go once medically cleared.

Don't ever give up – What was I supposed to do? Sit around my apartment feeling sorry for myself and waste my life away? Hell no! I didn't want anyone to feel sorry for me. It could've been worse. I'm lucky to be alive! I'll continue to fight and improve and be an inspiration for those who need it.

Evaluate – I checked in with my goals of time up in my chair and time exercising daily. If I achieved a goal one day, I rewrote the goal for the next session with an increase in time. If I met my goal for repetitions on a certain exercise, I crossed that off and increased the repetitions for the next workout. If I was having a bad day, maybe I was tired because of a poor night's sleep, I made sure to get to bed earlier so I could try to avoid this happening again.

BECOMING A PARALYMPIAN

Determine – I was provided an opportunity to be competitive, represent the USA on the highest level of amateur sport, and be a part of something bigger than myself.

Educate – What's it going to take to make this happen? It will mean more time away from my family. I'll need to ask for time off from work. This sport isn't entirely funded so how am I going to pay for the training and competition trips?

Create – My plan was to drive approximately 10 hour per week to get to a training facility and practice 4-5 times per week. I needed to have a physical workout routine in place to maintain my physical fitness. I also needed to have a mental routine in place to assist with training when off the ice. I had to organize a fundraiser to raise money to help offset the expenses I was going to incur and properly budget that money to last throughout the season. Since I was still teaching, I checked-in with my classes remotely from wherever I was in the world to monitor the progress of my students. I needed to ask the Board of Education for time off.

Implement – I found a long-term substitute teacher who best fit the needs of my students. Organized my fund raiser (secured location, DJ, collected raffle items, made up tickets, advertised, asked for donations for food and supplies). Approached Board of Education requesting time off to pursue Paralympics. Started physical and mental workouts with local trainers. Secured practice time.

Don't ever give up – At my first official Team USA training camp, I was told that with dedication on my part that I could earn a spot on the team. I stuck to my training schedule, as difficult as it was in many areas of my life. When I went to my first US Team Trials, I performed well enough to earn a spot on the team. The coach at the time was quoted in the paper saying that the only difference between me and the most veteran player on the team was practice time. That was all I needed to hear and that drove me to never give up.

Evaluate – At the end of the week, I checked in on my calendar to make sure I was putting in the training time I came up with when I was creating my plan. If I missed a day, I made sure to add another one on for the next week. I made sure I was doing some sort of physical and mental exercises 6 days a week. My fund-raiser was a huge success netting me more money than what I had hoped for. I budgeted that money for the season. The on-line monitoring of my students didn't go as well as I thought it would at first. I spoke with the parents of my students as well as my administration, and we changed our approach to make sure my students weren't impacted anymore.

At the age of 25, I was involved in an accident that changed my life forever. I lost the use of my legs. I'm lucky I didn't lose more. I'm fortunate to be paralyzed; how crazy does that sound? Before the accident, I was physically set in my life but wasn't mature mentally because I was never required to be. After the accident, it was all mental. Fortunately, with my inner drive and my incredible support system, I figured out how to mature mentally. I figured out how to get over my denial and allow the healing process to begin. It's okay to experience denial with any tragedy in your life.

I overcame my accident, as well as many other hardships in my life. I also turned a horrible incident into something positive with my success on the ice. I'm a proud US Paralympian. How have I overcome so much and become successful in life? People ask me all the time how did I do it? "If that were me, I don't think I could've done it." Garbage. Right away I tell them that until you're put in a situation like I was, waking up one day from a coma and being told that you'll never walk again, you don't know how you would react. We're all incredible human beings, and when presented with some drastic measures, we'll often surprise ourselves with how we respond. The main reason I had that defining moment in the pool in rehab was because I realized I needed to change my perspective on what happened. I decided to change my mindset and assign a different meaning to the accident. I no longer looked at the accident itself but now looked at it as an opportunity to turn everything around and somehow use it in my favor. I'm still alive. I can impact kids. I can impact people. I can inspire them and educate them to make better decisions.

I was immediately at peace with what happened, and I was on the road to recovery. As crazy as it may sound, I needed to self-assess, and

I believe everything happens for a reason. Bad things happen to good, strong people because we can handle it. It's a way to make us believe in ourselves when we overcome it.

So, to say that you don't think you'd be able to handle it is completely wrong. What else are you going to do? Crawl up into a ball and die? Although that happens all too often, it's not the way I was going to go. To me, it was a challenge. One that I was going to embrace and overcome and come out better than how I went in.

If you recall, we started this book talking about how important it is to have mentors in your life. Personally, I've had a dozen or so. Specifically, my mother and father, my high school coaching colleague Frank Schmidt, my college basketball coach Jim Calhoun, my physical therapist Carrie Silver Bernstein, my first curling coach Tony Colacchio, my girlfriend at the time of my accident Kim, Michael Jordan, and all of the nurses and doctors who guided my recovery along the way. There is no way I would be where I am in life today if it weren't for the many life lessons and knowledge that each of these people instilled in me.

My passion in life right now is to positively impact others and to lead them down the path to changing their lives, getting out of their own way, and allowing themselves to be happy and successful. That's what matters to me, teaching others to have the ability to overcome anything that's thrown their way. I've been through much in my life. I've grown. And I've learned. And now I'm sharing all of this with you.

Nobody is going to hand you success. It has to be earned by you and only you. Recognizing the fears you may have when faced with a certain situation is the first hurdle you must get over in order to conquer that fear. Successful people are not the ones who make the fewest mistakes. Successful people are the ones who are willing to make mistakes over and over and continue their journey. They don't let the mistakes deter them in any way from their final goal. In fact, they do the opposite. They embrace them and use them as learning tools and fuel to keep on going.

In his book, *Old School Grit. Times may change but the rules for success never do.,* Darrin Donnelly writes,

> "The people who achieve the most success in life are not those who somehow find a way to avoid making mistakes or encountering obstacles. No, mistakes and obstacles are an unavoidable part of life. The most successful people are those who are willing to keep moving forward after making mistakes. They find a way not to avoid life's inevitable obstacles, but to overcome them!" (Darrin Donnelly, Old School Grit)

You have to face your fears. You can't let a fear control your life any longer. Fears are nothing more than thoughts in our minds. They're not real. Fear is usually the number one deterrent to allowing change to happen. If you can master the idea that fear is only a thought and then overcome it, you will open yourself up to change. Fear causes so much negativity in our lives; it's sometimes difficult to overcome. But, like anything else, the more you do it, the easier it gets. Whatever your fear may be, jump right in and confront it with full force. You'll overcome it sooner than you think.

There may be a variety of reasons why you find yourself at a crossroads in your life where you need to decide to change. Are you complaining too much? Are you overthinking things? Maybe you're just in a rut and need to change your life. You need to stop taking life for granted. Everything you have right now in life could all be taken away from you at any given moment, in the blink of an eye. We have to appreciate every day and live it like it may be our last.

For the past 25 years, I've lived many experiences, traveled to many places, spoken in front of tens of thousands of people, and have spent a lot of time reflecting on my life. Every obstacle that's come my way I've always looked at as a challenge and an opportunity to get better. With the correct mindset, anybody can learn to take challenges in stride and always come out on top. But it takes time and training your mind to get that correct mindset. For me, it's easy. And if you follow The DECIDE Action Plan, you can train yourself to make those difficult decisions in life and either begin or continue to enjoy a successful, happy life.

This is the plan that I used. If you follow this process and put your heart into it, you'll have the best chance to succeed in the many difficult decisions that you'll face. It won't happen overnight. You won't start feeling the power of being your own hero right away but the more opportunities you have to put this action plan into place, the more successes you'll encounter. Over time, those successes will reshape your thinking about yourself. And you will eventually become your own hero.

However, if you choose to pick one or a couple of the steps and use them in any way you would like, you'll find yourself more informed and prepared to conquer what's in front of you. Or maybe it's just my story. Maybe something I went through, which helped me along my journey to where I am today, you can use in your life to overcome adversity or to make educated decisions moving forward.

Most decisions we make in our lifetime will come and go with virtually no altering consequences. The larger ones, however, will impact our lives forever, and those are the ones we'll remember. Every one of our decisions is composed of actions and consequences. I wanted to share my life and my process with you so that the consequences that go with the actions are the ones that you want and planned for. For me, the actions of drinking and driving brought consequences that changed my life forever.

What you do after the consequence is going to define who you truly are as an individual. Go ahead; make the decision. We're all going to have extreme stress. We're all going to be challenged in different areas of our lives. The ability to make that decision, the one that's right for you, will shape you and your legacy.

Every day, we're going to succeed and fail. Don't fear failure. You need to embrace it. It's going to happen. And when it does, you'll learn from it. Perfection doesn't exist in life. As long as you think it does, you're holding yourself back. Once you understand it doesn't exist, you'll treat yourself a little better and feel better about yourself. We all make mistakes. All of us were wrong at one time or another. As long as you attempt to correct what you did wrong and learn from it, you'll be successful. Stop trying to be perfect. Our differences are one of the many things that make us beautiful as individuals. This world would be a boring place if we were all the same. Keep in mind that winners aren't the ones who are always correct and never fail. Winners are the ones who are always learning and refuse to quit. If you're succeeding, stay humble and continue traveling the path you're on. If you're failing, stay hungry and learn from what you're doing wrong.

Learn to love yourself and know that only you can make yourself feel special. No one else. When you do this, you can power yourself to achieve great things. Everything you need to succeed is within you. Congratulate yourself and take pride in what you've accomplished. Compliment yourself daily. Talk yourself up! To be truly happy in life, you need to be 100% in love with yourself. If you're not, you need to change that. We cannot grow as individuals and help others in our lives until we truly love ourselves. Even after you change your attitude about yourself, and can honestly say that you love yourself, you'll still have some days or times when you may feel beaten down and lost. But those instances when you're having a bad day will be just that: a bad day. You'll feel so great about yourself that you won't allow yourself to let these feelings fester and grow. You can shut them down and not give them the attention they're looking for. When these "off" days happen, you need to fight extra hard to keep your overall goal in mind and keep striving for change. You'll eventually get there. During these times, you need to constantly remind yourself that the tough times won't last. You're too strong to allow them to last. You'll do something about them and make change for yourself. The path I was on in college with alcohol and stupid decisions was leading me toward alcoholism, toward a very scary place. Everyone has an addiction of some sort. Regardless, you're the hero of your own life and you can overcome anything in your way.

Who is your hero? The answer better be YOU! Get out of your comfort zone. Do you have the strength inside of you to be courageous and adventurous and try new things? I believe you do. Trying new things will allow you to fail and, therefore, learn and educate yourself. If we don't get out of our comfort zone and dare to dream, all the dreams inside of us will stay locked up and we'll lead mediocre lives. Live to the fullest and be your own champion.

***Don't forget...there's a free gift waiting for you.
Go to https://www.subscribepage.com/
youdecide and download it today***

Self-Publishing School

NOW IT'S YOUR TURN

Discover the EXACT 3-step blueprint you need to become a bestselling author in as little as 3 months.

Self-Publishing School helped me, and now I want them to help you with this FREE resource to begin outlining your book!

Even if you're busy, bad at writing, or don't know where to start, you CAN write a bestseller and build your best life.

With tools and experience across a variety of niches and professions, Self-Publishing School is the only resource you need to take your book to the finish line!

DON'T WAIT

Say "YES" to becoming a bestseller:

https://self-publishingschool.com/friend/

Follow the steps on the page to get a FREE resource to get started on your book and unlock a discount to get started with Self-Publishing School

ABOUT THE AUTHOR

Steve Emt knows what it takes to overcome difficult experiences.

Following an adolescence which saw Steve face adversities and accomplish great successes, his life was upended by an automobile accident at the age of 25 that left him confined to a wheelchair. Faced with the challenges of learning how to live again, Steve went on to finish college, earn his teaching and coaching degrees, and represent his country at the 2018 Paralympic Games.

He is now an accomplished public speaker empowering people to believe in themselves and become the hero of their own lives. The success Steve has achieved in managing life's difficult decisions has inspired him to share his formula in his first book, *You D.E.C.I.D.E.*.

Today, Steve splits his time with his family, training for Team USA and impacting others through coaching, mentoring and his public speaking engagements.

I'm begging you!

Thank You for Reading My Book!

I really appreciate all your feedback, and I love hearing what you have to say.

I need your input to make the next version of this book and my future books better.

Please leave me an honest review on Amazon letting me know what you thought of the book.

Thanks so much!

Stephen Emt

Made in the USA
Middletown, DE
24 November 2020